THE FUN KNOWLEDGE ENCYCLOPEDIA 2

ENCYCLOPEDIA 2

The Crazy Stories Behind the World's Most Interesting Facts

Trivia Bill's General Knowledge

BILL O'NEILL

DON'T FORGET YOUR FREE BOOKS

Contents

Introduction 1

Humans Didn't Invent Glue 2

The Angel's Share 2

A Haircut and Some Bloodletting Please............................ 3

Romeo, Romeo, Where's My Balcony? 3

Penicillin and the Dodgy Fruit 4

Hip-Hop and a Power Shortage 5

But He Doesn't Have a Monocle? 6

Hello, Clarice.. 7

Liquid Nitrogen Can't Freeze You...................................... 7

Explosives Cannot Be Detonated by Shooting Them 8

Buried in a Pringles Can 9

The Furby Spy?... 10

Have You Ever Wondered? 10

So That's Why He was the Unabomber? 11

Petunia Egeo 11

McDonald's in Blue?... 12

The Alternative 7 Dwarves.. 13

Shaggy has a Real Name.. 13

So, That's Where Duffel Bags Come From? 14

Barbie and Weight Loss Advice 15

Orange Does Have a Word That Rhymes....................................... 16

Saddam Hussein and Detroit 16

Lobster Wasn't Always a Delicacy 17

The Origins of Crayola 18

Failure to Predict the Future.. 18

An Offer You Could Refuse.. 19

Commercials and Football Don't Mix... 19

The Hollywood Sign Never Used to Say That 20

A Billionaire from Books.. 21

A Fun Weekend for a Husband and Wife 22

Swearing Does Help 22

The Tale of Two Italians 23

Go to Ireland to Give Blood.. 24

Why Did Yeltsin and Clinton Laugh? 24

Be Glad We Don't Say Hello Like It.. 25

A Clean Shave 26

Quite an Odd Job 27

Can You Trust a Doctor?.. 27

Nutella and Rations... 28

How Much on an Engagement Ring?... 28

But Women Can't Do That!!! 29

That's a Lot of Blood Vessels... 30

We All Eat the Same Chicken.. 30

If You Want to Write a Novel... 31

Surviving Not One But Two Bombs...31

George Lazenby Wasn't Actually an Actor..............................32

New Yorkers are More Dangerous than Sharks.....................33

The Spanking Slapper 33

Why Do the Sun and Moon Look the Same Size?..................34

Be Glad Humans Don't Do this Act 35

Cheese for Money 35

Why St Patrick's Day is So Boozy 36

Wizard Wizard 37

Smoked Bacon in War 37

Decisions, Decisions 38

That's a Bit Rich..39

Poor Mary..39

Hands Up for the Dummy 40

Do Shakespeare in its Real Voice 40

Stephen Hawking Keeps on Going..41

Mountain Dew and Mice 42

What a Bright Spark 42

Well, That's a Dead Cert 43

Well, this is Unfriendly 44

Twister isn't a Game..44

Imagine Terminator without Arnie 45

Now, That is Ambidextrous..45

Could You Believe there are Initials on the Moon? 46

Do You Want Coffee in the Office? 46

Poor Kitty 47

You Can Still Duel 47

Pointing the Direction.. 48

Beer as a Soft Drink? 49

Snow is Like Magic for Most... 49

A Psycho Melon... 50

A Different Olympic Games... 50

Don't Stop that Sneeze.. 51

Your Shoes Better Be Made for Walking................................. 51

Can You Really Trust a Raisin?... 52

Is it Me or am I Shorter? 52

That is a Big Yawn... 53

Somebody Give Him a Fright 53

Do You Want to Breathe in the Subway?................................. 54

Well, That's a Clean Giraffe... 55

Pope John Paul II and Basketball... 55

Fortune Cookies aren't Chinese.. 56

That Flea is for the High Jump 56

If Only the Names Had Stayed 57

Watch Out for the Deadly Coconuts.. 57

What are the Chances? 58

Your Eyes 58

And You Sleep on it 59

Colonial Africa 60

I Can See but Can't Think 60

Heroin Used to be Trademarked 61

That's a Lot of Bites 61

Watch Out when Left-Handed 62

How Fast to Become a Millionaire? 62

How to Understand Statues Involving a Horse 63

That is a Long Tapeworm 64

That is a Heavy Gut 64

Pubic Hair Causes Damage 65

Sticky Chewing Gum? 65

What a Fart Bubble 66

We Shed a Lot 67

Is Sherlock Holmes Real? 67

The Irish Population and the Potato Famine 68

The Great Pacific Garbage Patch 68

Are You Related to Genghis Khan? 69

Twins Born Days Apart? 69

Pac-Man and Pizza 70

Humans and Bananas 71

A Plague of Dancing? 71

Why Airplane Food Isn't So Good 72

Graffiti is Older than You Think 72

Fergie was Sally 73

How Much is that Art? 73

Land the Plane Now 74

Eating from the Toilet 75

What's the Time in Las Vegas? 75

Where Did the Island Go? 76

It's Nippy on Christmas Island 76

Don't Venture to Snake Island 77

That is a Big Family 78

A Kangaroo Looks Happy 79

Would You Like Some Cheese? 79

That's More Than Just a Step 80

The Village with No Roads 81

Imagine Having Blue Skin 81

The Red Ice 82

Cross-Border Opera 82

Well, That's a Different Toothpaste 83

A Gecko is the Real Spiderman 84

A Long Time to Hold Your Breath 84

Kiss My Donkey 85

Your Perfect Nap Time 85

Corn is the Global Product 86

That Fruit Looks Like an Ant 86

That is One Hungry Komodo Dragon 87

The Rule of Thumb Concept 88

The English-Speaking Chinese 88

Well, That Didn't Take Long..89

Happy Birthday to All of You 90

Getting Fat on Stamps 90

Urine Trouble Now Pussycat...91

You are Always Quite Close to the Sea in England 91

That Shrimp Packs a Punch...92

That Pigeon Loves its Art 92

Chicken Tikka Masala is Not Indian 93

As Drunk as a Chimp 93

Firefox isn't a Fox 94

Google and Their Goats 95

A Terrifying Crocodile 96

Is Bill Gates a Traitor? 96

The Queen of Swans...97

Not All Bats are Blind...98

This Fight Stinks!..98

That Sentence is for the Dogs.......................................99

A Cat Doesn't Have a Sweet Tooth 100

The Surfing Duck 100

That STD Has a Buzz about it.....................................101

The British and Their Tea 101

South Korea and the Turd 102

Men and Makeup..102

The Plastic Surgery Capital of the World.................................. 103

Your Brain is Faster than You Think...................................... 104

That is a Lot of DNA 104

You Really Have a Filthy Mouth 105

Tasting Faster than We Can See.. 106

The Whales with an Accent 106

The Cube Poop... 107

How to Keep Flies Away From You 107

The King with the Most Children... 108

Where Do Your Organs Come From? 108

Where Do Your Muscles Come From?.................................. 109

The Male Tank and the Female Tank.................................... 109

The Role of the Messenger Dog 110

Which War Claimed the Most American Lives? 111

Who Lost the Most Men in WW2? 112

How Did Egypt Get its Name? 112

The Problem with the Shortest Day of the Year.................... 113

The Most Expensive Olympic Games Ever 113

Who Invented Champagne?... 114

That is One Big Wedding.. 115

What is the Largest Snowman Ever Built?............................ 115

Who was the First American Serial Killer? 116

The Sociopathic Family 117

How Many Cars Exist on Earth? 117

Use Your Head when Opening Your Car 118

Keep Her Feet Warm 119

Why is Snow White in Color? 119

What is the New Car Smell? 120

What were the Youngest and Oldest Soldiers in the
American Civil War? 120

How the SS Took Items from Jews and Hid Them 121

The Monarch Butterfly Knows What It Likes 122

Why is it 007? 122

Anybody for Strawberries and Cream? 123

Who Used to Have Harrods Close Their Doors? 124

Who is the Real Robin Hood? 124

Imagine Writing this as Your Address 125

Where Does Halloween Come From? 126

Why Do You Cross One Finger? 127

What is Your Personal Bubble? 127

What are Non-Contact and High-Contact Cultures? 128

Do You Pacify with Your Behavior? 129

How Old is Your Greenhouse? 129

What Caused a Tulip Craze? 130

What Makes You More Attractive? 131

Where Does the Term 'Cosmetic' Come From? 131

How Big is Avon in Brazil? 132

Would You Do This to Remove Freckles? 132

What is the Most Popular Fruit in the World?........................ 133

Who was Responsible for the Hanging Gardens of
Babylon?.. 134

Why Does Lamborghini Have Such Strange Names?........... 134

Your Nails Say It All 135

Bleeding for Beauty 136

What is the Face Platter? 136

Does Your Lipstick Represent Social Standing? 137

Who was the First Person to Die in a Car Accident in the
United States?... 138

Would You Visit the Poison Garden? 139

A Fig Might Not Be Vegan... 140

What Terms are Fruits and Vegetables?................................ 140

How Many Copies of the Bible are Sold Each Year? 141

How Big a Problem was the Black Death?............................. 141

Do You Know Why Italy is Called Italy? 142

Bodies as Missiles 143

How Does Eyeshadow Glimmer? 144

What is the Coldest Temperature Ever Recorded? 144

How Old is Caffeine?.. 145

You Don't Actually Need Caffeine to Start the Day 146

That Cure has a Bad Smell... 146

What is the Worst Political Slogan Ever?............................... 147

Introducing the Hornet Bomb... 148

Where Does Money Come From? 149

The Eagle on the Silver Dollar 149

Which Drug is Most Widely Used? 150

How Many Deaths Do People Believe Happened in the
Bible? 150

What is the Bloodiest Battle in History? 151

Keeping People Out of the Vatican...152

Soda and Getting Older 152

Watch Out, Your Soda is on Fire...153

How Many Types of Tea Do You Believe Exists? 153

What is the Difference in Water Usage Between Africa
and the United States?...154

How Long Does It Take for a Plastic Bottle to
Decompose? 155

How Much More Expensive is Bottled Water Compared
to Tap Water?...155

What is the Complete Name of Pablo Picasso? 156

Was Cocaine Ever Sold on the Open Market?.........................157

What are the Origins of Chess? 157

The Meaning of the Himalayas 158

What are the Roots of Modern Day Vegetarianism?.............158

How Much Money was Lost on Black Tuesday?....................159

Walt Disney and Menstruation 160

How Many Tampons Will a Woman Use in Her Lifetime?
....160

Would a Wolf Make a Good Guard Dog? 161

What is the Legend of the Black Eyes on a Panda? 162

What is the Fastest Bear in the World? 162

A Guinea Pig is Not a Pig 163

Why Does Rudolph Have a Red Nose? 164

Mistletoe Might Not Be as Nice as You Think 164

More Books By Bill O'Neill 167

Introduction

The world is a fun and interesting place, and you never know the strange facts and theories that you can come across next. That is exactly what this book is all about; from bringing to you some of the most bizarre facts you can ever dream of, to other facts that may make you feel all warm and cuddly inside, to others that stop you in your tracks.

No matter if it is the reason as to why Rudolph has a red nose, the explanation of where the word 'money' comes from, or even the link between Walt Disney and menstruation. Yes, this fun-filled book has it all.

Contained within the pages are facts linked to technology, religion, the world—the range of subjects goes on and on. So, delve right in because the world of amazing facts is just waiting to be discovered.

Humans Didn't Invent Glue

Glue is pretty cool, and it is certainly something that is very useful in a number of ways, but did you know that humans (as we know them) were not the inventors? Instead, archaeologists have discovered that the first-ever version of glue was created by the Neanderthals approximately 200,000 years ago.

We aren't quite sure exactly how they made it, as there are several different options, but it seems that they used a type of tar that was manufactured from the birch tree. It even seems complicated to us at this moment in time, so you can only imagine how tough it was all of those years ago. Okay, it might have been rudimentary glue, but it still worked and held the dangerous part onto the wooden shaft of a spear for hunting, so it was still pretty important.

So, the next time you use glue for anything, just give thanks to a species that has not existed for tens of thousands of years because without them who knows where we would be today.

The Angel's Share

Scotland and whisky go together like, well Laurel and Hardy or any other famous double act that you care to imagine, but the chances are that you have never heard of something called 'The Angel's Share'. This is one thing that every distillery is aware of, and it is all to do with the way in which whisky is left to mature in wooden casks for years.

As each year passes, there is a certain amount of whisky that seeps through the wood and evaporates. On average, 2% is lost each year, but it does vary depending on the type of cask that has been used for storage. Tradition states that as this whisky vanishes into the heavens, it then leads to a series of rather drunk angels, which is in itself quite a cool thing to think about. However, it is actually an important part of the entire whisky making process since the maturation stage helps to remove some of the more undesirable aspects of the whisky, leading to something that is certainly much easier to drink.

We should really thank the angels for taking all of the bad stuff for their own selves.

A Haircut and Some Bloodletting Please

Have you ever found yourself looking at that red-and-white-striped pole that sits in front of a barbershop–and wondered where it came from? Well, the answer is back in history when a barber could not only cut your hair but also perform a range of medical procedures.

In particular, they would perform some bloodletting in an attempt to heal the sick, so you were kind of getting two for the price of one. Of course, the red on the pole represents blood while the white represents the bandages that they would then use to wrap you up afterwards. So, the next time you go to your barbershop, just remember to stick to the haircut or you might get more than you bargained for.

Romeo, Romeo, Where's My Balcony?

Whenever you think of Romeo and Juliet, what is the one scene that stands out in the mind of every single individual that has ever heard the story? That's right, the balcony scene when Juliet is shouting out for Romeo. It's so romantic.

But there's a problem.

The problem is that Shakespeare never even mentioned a balcony in the original play, and yet it has found its way into every play and movie that has existed since the 17th century, especially in modern adaptations. Instead, what has happened is that people have inserted a scene that originally appeared in a 17th century play by Thomas Otway.

In that play, called 'The History and Fall of Caius Marius' Otway ripped off the work by Shakespeare and threw in a balcony scene just to be different. Over the centuries, aspects of the two have somehow become entwined resulting in the balcony scene appearing in productions of Shakespeare's play, with which we are all familiar with today.

Oh, and furthermore, nobody had even heard of a balcony back in the days of Shakespeare, so unless he was able to time travel, it would have been impossible for him to write about it.

Penicillin and the Dodgy Fruit

Penicillin has literally been a lifesaver since it was discovered back in the 19th century by Alexander Fleming. However, he does not deserve all of the credit for the discovery because he was actually coming up short with his attempts to study mold.

He discovered it by accident, but the levels he was originally producing were insufficient for it to be of any use to anybody. Thankfully for him, along with the rest of the world, his assistant inadvertently came to the rescue.

One day, Mary Hunt brought a cantaloupe into the lab for no specific reason other than she had just picked it up from a shop. Upon cutting it open, Fleming saw that it was covered in a golden mold, and as a result of this examination, he discovered that it was a form of *Penicillium* that was able to produce over 200 times more penicillin than he had been able to do up until that point.

In other words, the millions upon millions of people that have been saved due to penicillin can give thanks to Fleming as well as the shop that was guilty of selling that rotten cantaloupe.

Hip-Hop and a Power Shortage

Hip-Hop is huge, and it is crazy to think about how much money is generated as a direct result of this music, but a lot of people don't realize that we have a power shortage to thank for it exploding onto the scene.

The place is New York City and the time is 1977. The city had a number of issues with high crime levels, a major recession was just drawing to an end, and race relations were also pretty poor. Underneath, there was a bubbling level of frustration and, as was the norm, people would turn to music to help.

Hip-Hop was just starting out, but very few of the people who were interested in it and wanted to get involved could afford the equipment. It was a music movement that was struggling to get going, but that would change on July 13, 1977.

In the midst of a hot and sweaty summer, a single lightning bolt managed to hit a power transmitter that left Long Island without power for 25 hours. It led to an explosion of anger and riots with over 1,600 stores being looted in a single day.

So, how does this relate to Hip-Hop exploding onto the scene?

Well, via the looting, a lot of DJ equipment and other musical items made their way into the hands of those that could not afford them before the riots. Suddenly, more people had the equipment to make the music that they wanted, so it's no surprise that shortly after the riots had come to an end, this new musical genre exploded onto the scene.

Maybe that lightning strike was the best thing to happen to music?

But He Doesn't Have a Monocle?

Monopoly is one of the most popular board games that has ever been created, and this popularity has led to a number of variations hitting the shelves across the world. Aside from the game, the character that appears on the box, called Rich Uncle Pennybags, has also become a cult figure.

But then, he is also a cult figure that people have constantly made mistakes with, which kind of shows how much attention we tend to pay to people.

Dear Uncle Pennybags has become a popular party costume, and people have a tendency to dress up in the exact same way with a top hat, a moustache, and a monocle. All sounds familiar, doesn't it?

Well, there's a problem with that costume. The problem is that our rich uncle has never had a monocle, and nobody knows why or where this phenomenon started. (Although some link it to a character that is a peanut and wearing a monocle, which is in itself a bit strange.)

If you don't believe us, go and dig around that cupboard to find the Monopoly game that was sitting there and pay close attention to the box. Do you see a monocle? Well, if you are thinking that his design has changed and that it would have originally been different, then think again. Instead, the design has stayed the same since he first appeared back in 1936.

Come back to this book after you have checked this fact out because you know you are very tempted to do so.

Hello, Clarice

Ah, 'The Silence of the Lambs' is one of those movies that was able to send shivers down the spines of every single individual that watched it, and there's no doubt that it was a phenomenon when it came out. There are so many scenes that stand out, and it also has its fair share of iconic lines that people can recite over and over again.

One such line, and this is something that has made it onto fan sites, newspapers, and even merchandise, is the line 'Hello, Clarice'-and you might even remember it.

If you do, then your mind is tricking you into believing something that was never said in the movie at any point. Yep, it's all a figment of your imagination, and you have been caught up in the excitement and tension that surrounds the movie in general.

Instead, he says 'Good Evening, Clarice' in the movie, but people that have seen the movie a number of times will still quote the line incorrectly. In fact, what is going on is that people have taken a line from another movie and mixed it together, but it has now become such a part of the history that later versions, including a TV series, now says those immortal words perhaps just to stop people from feeling that they have all made a huge mistake.

Liquid Nitrogen Can't Freeze You

There have been several movies where the bad guy has been killed thanks to being covered in liquid nitrogen resulting in them being frozen to the spot. It was even used in Terminator 2.

However, the problem with this approach is that being hit by a blast of it will not kill you. Actually, it's just going to make you a bit cold. You see, it won't do anything to you, and it is used by some in different forms of therapy to help treat a number of ailments, so if it was as deadly as the movies tried to make out, then why would it be used in that way?

Now, we aren't saying that you should go and start playing around with it, but there's no doubt that the substance is far milder than you were perhaps initially aware, but then who has some liquid nitrogen lying around in the first place?

Explosives Cannot Be Detonated by Shooting Them

Both movies and video games have created this idea that you can detonate explosives simply by shooting them. Let's face it, this does make for a pretty cool scene, and there is a certain sense of satisfaction when you manage to blow stuff up and run onto the next level.

The problem is that this is all absolute make-believe. It is a figment of the imagination of both the video game developer and the movie director because it just does not work that way in real life.

Explosives are actually quite stable, as they need to be in order to reduce the chances of them exploding by accident, resulting in people being hurt or killed. If you think of the movie Rush Hour where Tucker is shooting at a car that contains C4 that ends up blowing up as a good example of how Hollywood portrays it. But let's look at what really happens.

C4 may sound deadly, but it is one of the more stable explosive compounds around. You can shoot it, and it will do absolutely nothing as it requires a complex chain of events to occur, and a bullet being fired at it just doesn't do the trick.

But it goes further than that because you can also set fire to C4 and it will still not explode, although this is not something that we recommend trying out at home. The only way that you can shoot at explosives and detonate them is if you were able to hit a very specific and small part of the detonator, but the chances of that happening are so slim that it would need to be an absolute fluke shot for it to happen.

Buried in a Pringles Can

Pringles, everybody loves them, and their can is also pretty famous all over the world. However, surely being buried in a Pringles can is taking things to a whole new level?

Well, for most people that would certainly be the case, but it's different when you are the individual that was responsible for designing the iconic container? After all, would you not want to go that extra step and become immortal, buried in the very thing that you designed?

The man in question was Frederic Baur, and back in 1966 he came up with the idea of using a can to allow chips to be stacked on top of one another. This was different than the rest of the versions available at the time, which involved the standard bag, and it helped to make the Pringles brand what it is today.

Upon his death in 2008, at the age of 89, his sons managed to fulfill a request that he had made back in the 1980s, which was to have his ashes buried in a Pringles can. While everyone thought it was a joke, Frederic was dead serious about it, so while on their way to the funeral home after his death, his sons bought a can. What flavor? Well, they argue that it had to be original.

This was one case where he did indeed pop and then had to stop.

The Furby Spy?

At one point in our not too distant past, Furbies were an absolute phenomenon. Kids all over the world—and also a surprising number of adults—loved these toys, and you can only imagine how much money the people behind the craze were making.

However, not everyone was happy with them being brought along.

Take the NSA, for example. They were highly suspicious of these toys to such an extent that they were banned from being brought into their headquarters in Maryland. Their fear was that they would absorb secrets and then blurt them out later when they weren't in a secure environment. In other words, it was a cause for national security that Furbies were banned from the property.

But then, it does make you wonder why on earth someone would have taken them into their place of work to begin with. Don't they have enough work to do that they would resort to playing with toys when they were supposed to be keeping the country safe?

Have You Ever Wondered?

Chances are that you have used the term jaywalker on numerous occasions, but it's one of those words that just doesn't make sense, as it never seems to relate to what it is describing. So, you are probably thinking that it stems from the origins of the word, and you would be right.

However, the origins are not going to be what you would expect, as it never involved anybody called Jay.

Instead, the word 'jay' used to be the slang word for someone who was seen as being a 'foolish person, so when an individual was observed ignoring street signs, it seemed logical to combine jay with the word 'walker.' Ultimately, that is who it means 'a foolish walker, so now you can sleep easy and not feel as perplexed when you next use the term.

So That's Why He was the Unabomber?

Ted Kaczynski became infamous due to him becoming known as the Unabomber. For years, he terrorized people across the United States, and it took a prolonged period of time to track him down and finally put his evil campaign to rest.

But even though it is quite common for criminals such as him to be given names, the idea of the 'Unabomber' is something that is often confusing to people. However, the explanation is more basic than we are perhaps willing to concede.

In fact, the theory behind him being called the Unabomber simply stems from the locations of his first attacks. At the outset, his main focus was on Universities and Airlines, so it was hardly a giant leap of the imagination to take the UN from universities and A from airlines to ultimately result in the use of UNAbomber.

There, we said it was easier to understand than you expected.

Petunia Egeo

The Vatican is huge. It is also a place where tradition has the habit of hanging around for centuries and potential change is slow. Furthermore, the Vatican also has a number of different departments that all add up to what is, for them, daily life.

The Vatican bank is one part of the institution that has

11

certainly embraced change even though its intricate dealings still remain a mystery to many. But, in one area where they believed that technology could be useful is with the installation of ATM machines where members of the Vatican bank can do all of the things via an ATM that we are used to doing anywhere else in the world.

However, there is one difference.

You have to remember that part regarding change being slow, and this is not different. It seems that they just cannot let go of certain aspects that they believe make them stand out from the rest. What are we talking about? Well, the ATM machines connected to the Vatican bank are the only ones in the world that offer you Latin as an option when it comes to the language that is displayed on the screen.

Now, where did we put that Google translate?

McDonald's in Blue?

When it comes to logos that are famous around the world, the golden yellow arches of McDonald's must rank as one of the best. As soon as you see the top of an arch, you know instantly what it is that you are looking at, and it is a color that is seen at every single McDonald's around the world from Seattle to Shanghai.

Well, everywhere apart from one single location.

Now, you might think that the location would be in some strange country where they just don't get the concept of McDonald's, but you would be incorrect. Instead, the location is right there in the United States.

Head to Sedona, Arizona, and there you will find that their McDonald's has used a pale blue color for the famous arches rather than yellow. You would think that this would outrage McDonald's as it is all part of their branding, but that doesn't seem to be the case.

Instead, the city government had already banned the use of yellow when they granted permission for the McDonald's to open, and it was all down to how they wanted to preserve the city. In Sedona, there is a lot of natural red rock, and the city government thought that the yellow arches would just not work against that backdrop, resulting in them making the owners change it to turquoise.

Somehow, the idea of it all being turquoise just doesn't seem right.

The Alternative 7 Dwarves

Who doesn't love the Disney classic characters, the 7 dwarves? However, even though the names of the final seven are quite well known, Walt Disney did have a number of other names under consideration during production.

Some of the alternative options that were floating around included names such as: Wheezy, Burpy, Tubby, and even Deafy, which would have been seen as absolutely horrific in the world today. You have to admit that those kinds of names just didn't have the correct ring about them, so it was best that they chose those names that we have all come to love and adore.

Shaggy has a Real Name

Scooby Doo has been an insanely popular cartoon since it first hit our screens back in 1969. Since then, it has gone through a number of different incarnations, but there's no doubt that it has brought a lot of fun and enjoyment to many people, both kids and adults alike.

However, it is not just Scooby Doo that is popular, even though he is the coolest character of them all. His human sidekick, Shaggy, is also recognized as being one of the cool cats in the show. His unkempt appearance, cowardly approach to pretty much anything, and 'zoinks!!' catchphrase has led to him having real appeal with the audience, but then we all know him simply as Shaggy.

What most people are not aware of is that Shaggy is not his real name, even though it is the one thing that everybody knows him by. So, what is the real name for this fictional character? Well, it's the decidedly boring Norville Rogers, and you must admit that it would never have had the same impact compared to being called Shaggy. Sometimes a nickname really does work out for the best.

So, That's Where Duffel Bags Come From?

Who hasn't at least heard of a duffel bag? Come to think of it, who hasn't either owned one or known someone that has owned one? If you don't fall into any of those categories, then you are going to be in the absolute minority.

However, the duffel bag is another prime example of an object for which we often have no real understanding where it comes from. After all, duffel sounds like a strange word that to many makes no sense whatsoever. Well, when you actually research the origins, you discover that it is far more straightforward and easy to understand than you would expect.

In fact, the name 'duffel bag' simply comes from the town in Belgium that was the first to supply the materials that were then used to create the finished product. That town was called Duffel, so the manufacturer decided just to keep that name as a kind of homage to the important role that it played in getting things to market. Now, does that not make you start to think about other things and whether their name stems from a real place?

Barbie and Weight Loss Advice

It is believed that there have been over 1 billion Barbie dolls sold since they made their appearance back in 1959. Since then, she has become more than a cult icon, and the brand has expanded into more formats with Barbie herself appearing in various styles.

However, one style and doll that appeared in the 1960s was certainly different, and it included some advice that we would just be completely shocked at if it was aired today.

The doll in question was Slumber Party Barbie, and if you were a lucky enough girl to receive this version, then you would have also been given a surprise book that titled 'How to Lose Weight.' Now, that in itself is shocking enough when you consider the age range of the market that it was being aimed at, but one of the tips in particular goes beyond shocking.

So, what is the tip? Surprisingly enough, they gave the tip to the girls who wanted to lose weight and read the book, that they should simply not eat. Plain and simple. If you want to lose weight, then avoid food.

To be honest, should you be taking weight loss advice from a plastic doll?

Orange Does Have a Word That Rhymes

There is a widely held belief that the word 'orange' does not have anything that rhymes with it. Actually, this is a question that is often used in trivia competitions, as people just believe that it is a unique word in the English language.

But there's a problem if you just fall into the trap of believing that it is unique. The truth of the matter is that there is one word that rhymes, and that word is 'sporange.'

Now, admittedly that does sound like a word that is just made up and cannot really exist, but it does. The word comes from botany, and it means 'spore case' which is why you have probably never heard of it before. The good thing is that you now have the correct answer to give the next time that someone asks you to think of something that rhymes with orange, and you'll leave people amazed that an answer does indeed exist.

Saddam Hussein and Detroit

Considering he has now gone down in history as one of the worst dictators in the history of the world, it seems absolutely bizarre to discover that there is a link between Saddam Hussein and Detroit.

Famous for running Iraq throughout the 1980s and 90s, as well as killing who knows how many people that tried to oppose him, including Kurds against whom chemical weapons were used, we all know what eventually happened to him. However, his story is a prime example of how times can really change.

Back in 1980, he was certainly not regarded by the US as being the kind of person that they should be wary of. In fact, he was kind of seen as being on the good side as opposed to the likes of Iran, so it's fair to say that there were a number of things going on behind the scenes that the public were not aware of.

But one city went further than any of the rest, and that city was Detroit.

Rather unbelievably, the city presented Saddam Hussein with the keys to the city, which is a pretty impressive honor to bestow on someone. It does make you wonder as to what they then thought a few years later when it all started to go wrong.

Lobster Wasn't Always a Delicacy

If you go into a seafood restaurant and order lobster, you know that it is more than likely going to hit you hard in the pocket. It is for that single reason that eating lobster is often reserved for a special occasion where you don't mind pushing the boat out a bit.

However, rather surprisingly, this has not always been the case, as can be seen if you venture back into the earliest days of Colonial America. At that time, lobster was so plentiful that you wouldn't just walk into a place that sold them and see a few in the tank with you then making your decision. Instead, they were so bountiful that they were actually fed to prisoners—which you would never imagine happening in the world today.

Just imagine the uproar if prisons around the world were feeding the inmates things such as lobster, and yet back in colonial times, it was seen as being nothing unusual. For us, eating lobster on a regular basis hardly sounds like a punishment, so it just shows how times have indeed changed so much.

The Origins of Crayola

Crayola is one of those brand names that just stands out from the crowd, and they certainly dominate their own particular market. However, it is also one of those names where you can perhaps sit and wonder as to what the origins are since it does, at first, appear to be a nonsensical name.

But, as in most cases, the explanation itself is far more straightforward to understand than you would perhaps expect. For this, we need to go to France in order to get to the root of Crayola.

The rather simple explanation is that it combines two different French words, 'craie' and 'ola' and the literal translation means 'oily chalk'. It means this because the 'craie' part means chalk, and 'ola' translates as oily. When you look at it from that perspective, then it really is pretty easy to see how a small leap in the imagination led to the creation of the name 'Crayola.'

Failure to Predict the Future

We all know that the iPhone has been one of the most amazing inventions of recent times. The market share that it has been able to capture is pretty impressive, and each new incarnation leads to queues around the block as people wait patiently to get their hands on the latest version.

With its success, you would perhaps find it hard to believe that not everyone in the technology industry was convinced. Enter right of stage, Steve Ballmer who, in 2007, was the CEO of Microsoft. Now, you would imagine that the CEO of a technology giant such as Microsoft would be pretty up-to-date on trends and the way in which the market is going, but it seems that this was not the case.

Upon the release of the iPhone, Ballmer was directly quoted as saying that "the iPhone would never be able to capture a share of the market." In other words, he was convinced that it was doomed to be an absolute failure.

So, Steve, how well did that prediction go?

An Offer You Could Refuse

When it comes to populous countries, China is the market leader with well over 1 billion inhabitants. If you thought that this was a relatively new phenomenon, then think again, because it seems that there have been population issues for decades.

Actually, it was something that was annoying to the Chinese leadership even when they were far more secretive than they are today. Even though information is difficult to come by, we do know of one incident in 1973 that involved an offer that the US simply had to turn down.

Back in 1973, the famous Henry Kissinger had an audience with Mao Zedong. During that meeting, Chairman Mao mentioned that China had far too many women compared to men. Ultimately, he suggested that he give the US 10 million Chinese women like some strange diplomatic gift that just beggars belief. Of course, Kissinger had to turn him down, because can you imagine going back to the President with 10 million women behind you? It just wouldn't work.

Commercials and Football Don't Mix

Have you ever spent time wondering about how finely tuned the link is between commercials and sporting events?

Everything appears to be down to a fine art, but that has not always been the case.

Of course, when something goes wrong, if you would think that the viewer at home would miss the start of the sporting event just because the commercial had managed to over-run, well you would be wrong.

Back in 1967, the Super Bowl was on the road to becoming the commercial success that you would imagine it would be. Advertising revenues were climbing, and for NBC there was a serious amount of cash to be made.

However, it seems that NBC perhaps got a bit greedy, which led to them having their commercials on for longer than intended. As a result, the viewers were still being advised on what to buy when the second half kicked off. You would have thought that this would be the end of it, but it seems that the power of advertising was too strong. Remarkably, officials told the Packers that they would need to start all over again simply because the viewers had missed it!

From that moment on, you can guarantee that the networks paid even closer attention to their commercials to make absolutely certain that nothing went wrong with their timing.

The Hollywood Sign Never Used to Say That

When it comes to signs in the world, it is perhaps fair to say that the Hollywood one is the most famous to have ever existed. It must have appeared in so many TV shows, movies, and holidaymaker snapshots over the years. For many, it is the symbol of the Hollywood dream of becoming a star, and indeed its significance in this area cannot be under-estimated.

So, people would be rather surprised to discover that the sign itself didn't always say just Hollywood.

Its origins stretch back to July 1923. On Friday 13th, there was an inauguration ceremony held in Griffith Park to commemorate the unveiling of a sign in Los Angeles. The sign was to represent the development of a residential setting by H.J. Whitely. Its name? Hollywoodland.

Yep, the sign that we now recognize as saying Hollywood used to have a 'land' part added on the end, and it also had nothing to do with the movie business whatsoever.

We have no idea when it lost the 'land' part of the sign, and we also have no idea when it came to represent Hollywood and the movie business. But then, can you now ever imagine it changing or standing for anything other than that Hollywood dream?

A Billionaire from Books

You would think that becoming a billionaire just from selling books would be impossible, and it almost is, as only one individual has managed to achieve this rather remarkable feat. Perhaps not surprisingly, that individual is the creator of the Harry Potter series, J.K. Rowling, who really did come from absolutely nowhere and created something that became a phenomenon.

However, she was only a billionaire for a relatively short period of time simply because she then proceeded to give away quite a lot of money to various causes and charities. It was this unselfish act that caused her to lose this status, but then when you have as much money as she does even after the charity acts, does it really make that much difference?

A Fun Weekend for a Husband and Wife

Do you ever find yourself a bit lost for something to do as a married couple at the weekend? Well, if that is indeed the case, then the perfect answer is sitting there right in front of you.

One weekend a year over in Finland, they get a number of happily married couples together for some frivolity. There are laughs all around, and the hope is that the couples are still happy together by the end of the day.

So, what do they actually get up to?

Finland is the location for the World Wife Carrying Championship, which does sound rather bizarre, but then when you see it in action it becomes even stranger than you could have ever imagined. Basically, the husband picks up his wife, who then hangs upside down with her legs around his neck (rather than her hands) while her head dangles down towards the ground. When they are ready, there is then a race to the end of the course to determine who can carry them the greatest distance.

But what is the prize for all of this, we hear you ask?

Well, just to make sure that the entire competition remains one-sided, the prize for the winner is beer. Yep, beer, and how much beer you are wondering? Well, that depends on the weight of your wife, as that is the deciding factor.

As we said, if you are bored one weekend, then maybe start training.

Swearing Does Help

There is this idea that swearing is just bad language and that there is no need for it at any point. However, while some choice words may not be pleasant on the ears of different individuals, research has shown that it may not all be as bad as you think.

Instead, what the research has unveiled is that swearing while you are in pain could actually prove to be beneficial for the individual who is in pain. It seems that the act of swearing magically releases pain-relieving endorphins, so whatever is hurting you will no longer appear to be as bad.

So, the next time you bang your toe on the chair leg or stand on that up-turned plug, just remember to swear, and the pain will all be over in next to no time at all.

The Tale of Two Italians

When it comes to luxury sports cars, the Ferrari seems to always be on a completely different planet to anything else that has existed. These cars are just seen as being so stylish, with new models being sold out before they are even finished coming off the production line.

However, they do have a competitor, and it is another Italian. The crazy thing is that it was due to Enzo Ferrari that the competitor even existed in the first place.

According to the story, Enzo Ferrari was in a discussion with a young man back in Italy. During that conversation, he was rather scathing about the man with him telling him how 'you may be able to drive a tractor, but you will never be able to handle a Ferrari properly.'

Now, you might be wondering why that phrase would have such an impact on the future of Italian sports cars, but it all changes when you discover that the man he said it to was none other than Ferruccio Lamborghini. So incensed at the insolence of the man, Lamborghini then decided that he would do anything he could to produce the best car in the world, and so the famous car was born.

Since that day, the two have been constantly battling one another for supremacy, and it was all because of one comment.

Go to Ireland to Give Blood

Giving blood is certainly a worthwhile event, and you may be familiar with getting a drink after it as you just lie there and wait to recover from the process. Well, if you want to do something a bit different, then you should consider going to Ireland in order to donate some of your own red liquid, as a tradition there does mean that they tend to do things a bit differently to other countries.

Ireland is, of course, the home of Guinness, so you can perhaps guess as to where this is now heading. It used to be the case that anybody giving blood in Ireland would then be given a pint of Guinness to help them to put the iron back in their body that they had lost when giving blood.

You can guarantee that when this first appeared that there would be queues around the block, and they would never have had a shortage of blood, not when there was free Guinness to be had.

Why Did Yeltsin and Clinton Laugh?

Relations between the United States and Russia have been a bit up and down since the end of the Cold War. However, if you throw your mind back to 1995 and a meeting between Boris Yeltsin and Bill Clinton, you can get an idea of how different things can be.

According to reports, there was one very important question on the mind of Yeltsin when he met Clinton for the first time. Was it about something that the US had done to upset the Russians? Was it about some other country? A diplomatic issue that could endanger the world once again and plunge us all back into the Cold War?

Nope.

Apparently, his first question was whether O.J. Simpson was guilty of killing his wife. Yep, the biggest media circus and murder mystery of perhaps all-time was the one thing that the Russian President wanted to know about the most.

We aren't sure as to what the answer was, as Clinton has never seemed to divulge that, probably for political reasons, but it does show how even leaders of countries are actually still normal people.

Be Glad We Don't Say Hello Like It

As you go around the world, there are various ways in which we can say hello to one another. The handshake, the nose rubbing, air kisses on the cheeks—they are all things that we will be familiar with.

But just be thankful for one moment that you are not a member of another species of the animal kingdom, the white-faced capuchin monkey to be precise.

You see, when two of them meet one another, they have a very peculiar way of saying hello, and it is something that is not replicated anywhere else in the animal world. They say hello by sticking their fingers up the nostrils of the other monkey.

Yep, you read that correct. They stick their fingers up the

nostrils of the other monkey.

Now, can you imagine us doing that when we see someone and want to say hello? Well, it could perhaps be worse.

A Clean Shave

When you look back in history at the best military leaders to have ever existed, Alexander the Great would have to be right up there pretty much at the top. His skills on the battlefield cannot be disputed, but could it be the case that he was able to achieve so much because of his amazing army, or did he pay particular attention to even the smallest of details?

To be honest, it was probably a bit of both, and if you are looking for evidence of that, then look no further than this little gem. According to sources from the time, Alexander the Great was concerned about the potential role that having beards could play on the battlefield. Remember, this was a time where they would not really wear helmets like they did in later centuries, so their beards would be there on full display.

Also, battles were fought in close quarters, and it was very much up close and personal, and this concerned Alexander. As a result, he ordered that every single soldier should shave off his beard, as this would stop the enemy from being able to grab onto them during battle giving them a rather unfair advantage.

On the other hand, it also perhaps gives you an indication of the kind of tactics that he would use, as he must have surely thought about it because his soldiers were guilty of doing the exact same thing. Well, all is not fair in either love or war.

Quite an Odd Job

Danny DeVito has been a popular actor for what feels like an absolute eternity. However, he has not always been in the movie business. He may have had his breaks way back in the 1970s, but before he was able to become famous, he did have a slightly more normal job.

Well, if we are being honest, there is nothing normal about his previous form of employment.

You see, little Danny, was a hairdresser. Nothing strange or peculiar about that, we hear you ask, but his customers were unable to complain about the finished job that he would do.

Mr. DeVito was actually a hairdresser for corpses rather than living humans. Now, that does make you wonder about how good a hairdresser he was if he was only allowed to work on those individuals that were already dead. After all, he could pick and choose their style as they could hardly say anything back to him.

Can You Trust a Doctor?

A kind of running joke is that you don't only need brains and intelligence to be a doctor, but you also need to be horrific at handwriting. However, it may be more of a problem than you are perhaps aware.

According to statistics, it is believed that poor handwriting of doctors results in the death of approximately 7,000 people in the United States each year. That in itself is crazy, and it makes you wonder about the way in which they end up dying. Wrong medication, the wrong amounts, not getting the correct treatment, and all because a doctor seems to have a natural habit of being unable to write in a style that is able to be read by anybody else.

Perhaps the next time you go to the doctor you should ask for them to type it out, just to be on the safe side.

Nutella and Rations

Nutella is a massive brand with millions of jars sold on an annual basis around the world. That small jar brings so much delight to everybody that dips into it, but few are aware of the way in which the product itself actually came to fruition.

To understand its origins, we need to head back to World War II, which was the time of rations. An Italian pastry maker was getting rather fed up of what amounted to rather meagre chocolate rations, and he wanted to do anything possible in order to extend it as far as he could. Ultimately, it led to him adding in some hazelnuts, as it was probably the only thing that he had lying around that made any kind of sense.

In other words, if it wasn't for rations during the war, Nutella would have never existed, at least not in the form that we all love. Perhaps there is at least one thing that we should be grateful for after all.

How Much on an Engagement Ring?

You may have heard the theory that a man should spend the equivalent of two months of his salary when buying his future wife her engagement ring. However, have you often wondered where this 'tradition' actually came from?

Now, guys could be sitting there thinking that it was all down to women who wanted a large and impressive ring, but that is not the case. Instead, the culprit is none other than de Beers'. If that name sounds familiar but you cannot quite place it, then it is the name of a famous diamond company, the largest in the industry.

Yep, you guessed it, this theory was all a marketing ploy to try to get guys to spend more money on a de Beers' product, as they thought that it was something they had to do in order to show their love. When you stop and think about it, this was quite a clever trick considering the way that it began to take hold, and men did indeed feel obliged to spend as much money as possible.

But Women Can't Do That!!!

In the world today, we are used to encountering female doctors of all kinds. It is nothing special, but it was clearly not always the case when you look back into history. In fact, the very first woman who was allowed to enter medical school from the United States was apparently admitted as a joke!

Yes, the men at Geneva Medical School thought that it would be a jolly good old laugh if they allowed this woman by the name of Elizabeth Blackwell into their hallowed halls. They believed that she would make a fool of herself, and it would prove some idea that women were just not able to work in these kinds of jobs.

However, the laugh really was on them, because after being admitted in 1847, she then graduated from medical school in 1849, much to the amazement of everybody else who was in her class. After that, she immediately sought to open her very own practice and ultimately went on to create an infirmary with the sole purpose of helping to look after the poor.

Once she had graduated, it's fair to say that attitudes towards women in the medical field changed quite considerably.

That's a Lot of Blood Vessels

Everybody knows that we need blood in order to survive. It flows around our body via an intricate roadmap of blood vessels that looks rather impressive when you see it drawn on a medical diagram.

But then, do you know how far your blood vessels would stretch if they were all laid out end to end?

Rather surprisingly, they would stretch for a total of 60,000 miles, which means they would wrap around the earth—twice! Clearly, this is only possible because of the small size of the vessels in your body, or else we would all be a crazy size, but it is just another example of how amazing the body is.

We All Eat the Same Chicken

When it comes to meat that is popular, then you would be hard pressed to find something that could surpass the popularity of chicken. However, even though there are millions and millions of them eaten around the world, you may not be aware that we are pretty much eating the same chicken.

Now, you could be confused as to what we mean here, so let us explain.

Back in 1948, there was a chicken competition that became known as the 'Chicken of Tomorrow' contest. Ultimately, the prize was something that was completely different, as it is now known that pretty much all of the chickens that we now eat today stem from the genetic code of the winner of that competition.

The genetics of that one single bird are now the dominant one to be found in poultry farms around the world.

If You Want to Write a Novel...

You have to admit, that when it comes to murder mystery novels, Agatha Christie is still one of the best that has ever lived. Her stories have been made into countless TV shows, TV movies, and millions of books sold around the world. Throw in plays, and you have a literary phenomenon.

Over her lifetime, she wrote a vast number of books, but you would perhaps wonder how on earth she could continue to have so much inspiration to continually produce things that were out of this world.

Well, it turns out that Agatha Christie herself gave us an insight into the kind of thing that helped her mind click into place. According to the author herself, she would come up with the best ideas while she was sitting in her bathtub eating apples. Now, we would like to think that she was actually having a bath at the time, as it would be strange to sit there clothed and eating an apple, but we have to leave that possibility open.

No matter if she was clothed or not, it did seem to do the trick, and we have a lot to be grateful for that she was able to come up with an idea that worked for her on a creative level.

Surviving Not One But Two Bombs

Being caught up in one bomb would be difficult, but imagine if you were unlucky enough to be caught up in two. Now, let's ramp this up to another level and say that you would need to be the unluckiest person alive if both of those bombs were atomic bombs that were dropped on Japan to end the war.

Well, there is one such man who did indeed end up being caught up in both of the bombs.

His name was Tsutomu Yamaguchi, and he found himself in

Hiroshima on a business trip when the bomb was dropped on the city. In shock, and having had a miraculous escape, he returned to his home in the city of Nagasaki.

Of course, the following day, the bomb was then dropped on Nagasaki, but amazingly he survived both and lived until the ripe old age of 93. It just seems as if there are some people that are really not supposed to be gone until it is their time no matter what they end up facing.

George Lazenby Wasn't Actually an Actor

You would think that being given the role of James Bond would only happen to those guys that had an established history in the world of acting. However, that's not the case when it comes to George Lazenby, the guy that ended up taking over the role from Sean Connery for the movie, On Her Majesty's Secret Service, in 1969. Prior to that, he had been in a few commercials and had been working in advertising as a model. Legend states that he was having a haircut in London and the guy sitting beside him was Albert Broccoli, who was the producer of the Bond series.

It is said that Broccoli recognized Lazenby from the commercials he had been in and made the decision that he could be a good Bond. Upon inviting him for a screen test, Lazenby then turned up dressed the part, including the Rolex watch. It seems that he managed to hit the mark, as he was then given the role but ultimately ended up making just the one movie. He said that the crew wouldn't listen to him because he had no acting background and his career pretty much collapsed after it.

It seems that one Bond movie was his highlight, and he was only ever really known then for being married to the tennis player Pam Shriver.

New Yorkers are More Dangerous than Sharks

Unless you stay in New York yourself, you may very well have the idea that New Yorkers are actually pretty dangerous. Well, it seems that this is kind of backed up by some studies even though the comparisons that are being drawn are perhaps not along the normal lines that you would expect to see.

In this instance, the comparison is between New Yorkers and sharks. Yes, you read that correct, sharks.

You would be forgiven for wondering how on earth you could ever have any kind of statistics that combine the two, but it has been done. You see, it has been uncovered that more people are bitten each year by New Yorkers than sharks. Yep, that is an actual fact, and you have to admit that it is quite a scary one when you stop and think about it.

So, the next time you are in the sea, remember to look out for both sharks as well as someone from New York, as you are in equal danger no matter who or what you encounter.

The Spanking Slapper

London has had a number of rather interesting characters throughout its history. Of course, most have heard of Jack the Ripper, but go back into the 1600s and you have another character who managed to send terror through the hearts and minds of those who resided in the city at that time.

However, this was not someone who would kill or maim their victims leaving them in a gory and bloody mess for somebody else to find. Nowhere near it.

Instead, some individual would stalk the streets of London

armed with a rod, and upon setting eyes on a potential victim would use their stealth to creep up on them before lashing out. Okay, it sounds a lot worse than it was because all he did was spank them with his rod while shouting out the term 'Spanko!' followed by him running off.

When you now stop and think about it, you can begin to see that this guy was just not in the same league as Jack the Ripper after all.

Why Do the Sun and Moon Look the Same Size?

When you look up into the sky and think of the sun and the moon, have you ever wondered how on earth they manage to look the same size? It clearly doesn't make any sense simply because you know that the sun is much larger than the moon, so it must be that your eyes are starting to fail on you or some strange trick of the light.

Well, the reason why they look the same size is because of something that is much stranger than your eyes starting to not work. It is all due to there being a strange coincidence.

You see, the moon is indeed smaller than the sun, much, much smaller. To be exact, it is 400 times smaller, but then how does that then correspond to it looking the same size as the sun in the sky?

Well, that is where the coincidence comes into play.

Not only is the moon 400 times smaller, it is also 400 times closer to the earth than the sun. It is that one single fact that then means everything is balanced out to such an extent that they do indeed appear to be identical in size.

Be Glad Humans Don't Do this Act

When it comes to getting their freak on, the animal kingdom has a number of ways in which the male and female prepare for the most intimate of acts. Some are quite impressive, with a funky dance showing off bright feathers, but other acts are just downright-strange.

Take the giraffe as a prime example. Now, most people struggle to work out how they are able to get things going in the giraffe bedroom department, but that is not what we are talking about. Instead, it is part of the mating ritual that is the strange point.

As they attempt to get each other in the mood, the male giraffe will come up to the female and rub up against her rather high-up bum. But that is still not the strange part.

He will keep on doing that until the female giraffe pees. But wait, that is still not it.

You see, the female doesn't just pee anywhere. Oh no, she pees into the mouth of the male giraffe. After that, it is action stations, as there is nothing that will get a male giraffe going than a female giraffe peeing in his mouth. Who needs Viagra in the giraffe world when you have that on tap?

Cheese for Money

People love cheese and the thousands of different varieties that are out there for you to indulge yourself with. However, the value of cheese takes on a completely different concept when you venture over to a part of Italy.

Credem Bank in Italy has a rather unusual method of collecting collateral for a loan. They don't look at your home, vehicle, or anything else as, for them, it is all about cheese.

However, they only seem to deal in one type of cheese, Parmesan. They accept cheese in return for loans that have interest rates between 3% and 5%, and they will then sell the cheese if the loan amount is not repaid within the time limit. They also charge a fee to make sure that the cheese will be able to mature correctly while it is in the bank vault. At the last count, they had 430,000 cheese samples in the vault, which has a market value of somewhere in the region of $200 million.

Why St Patrick's Day is So Boozy

St Patrick's Day appears to have been able to transcend being a national holiday in Ireland to becoming almost like a global party. Now, the one thing that it is certainly linked to is alcohol, and the answer is now linked to the fact that the Irish are rather fond of a drink or ten.

Nope, it is more to do with its origins and people in general taking advantage of it all.

At the outset, it was seen as being simply a feast day and was a time where Christians were allowed to celebrate and commemorate him, and in order to do so they could put aside the various restrictions on both food and alcohol that were linked to Lent.

In other words, religion decided that you could have some nice food and a few drinks on that day, but at the time there was no way of knowing that it would turn into what it has done now. To be honest, the food part has largely been left alone, but the same cannot be said for alcohol, as that is certainly being done to excess.

So, the next time you want to blame the Irish for this alcohol-filled day, stop yourself in your tracks and decide to blame the Christians instead.

Wizard Wizard

This piece of trivia is going to take some explaining, but it is going to be worth it all in the end.

There is something cool about a wizard, but the actual word itself does not get enough praise for just how cool it really is. You see, if you look at the word, it appears to be nothing too special, but that is until you do something a bit different.

Look at the W-I-Z-A-R-D part and then change the letters for their opposite ones in the alphabet, and something different happens. To explain it better. The letter A in wizard would be replaced by the letter Z and vice-versa.

If you do this with the letters in wizard, then what you end up getting is…...wizard just it is all in reverse.

Now, you have to admit that this is the kind of trivia thing that you have always wanted to learn.

Smoked Bacon in War

In ancient times, it was not unheard of for elephants to be used as instruments of war. You can imagine how the sheer size of them would be daunting to the enemy that had never set eyes on anything of this size before.

However, it seems that some armies came up with a plan to counter the elephant attack, and it does make you wonder as to how on earth they managed to conjure it up to begin with.

The plan focused on the use of pigs. Yep, pigs. It was

somehow discovered that the huge and impressive elephant was actually terrified of pigs, both in their appearance as well as that squeal. As a result, there was the idea that they should be sent into battle to basically scare off the elephants, but it is also known that some armies would go an extra step to make them even more intimidating.

It seems that some armies would set the pigs on fire and send them off to tackle those elephants. You have to admit that this then creates one crazy image of a pig on fire running towards an elephant which then charges in the opposite direction to get away from it.

Decisions, Decisions

Have you ever been in the situation where you are undecided about what to do, or what to choose, between two different options? If so, then you may very well have decided to put it down to chance and flip a coin. You choose heads for one option and tails for the other, and it seems a fair way to settle things once and for all.

However, spare a thought for an English composer by the name of Jeremiah Clarke.

Poor Jeremiah had decided that he was going to commit suicide, but as he stood at the side of a lake he was unable to decide if he would do so by either hanging himself or going into the water and drowning. Due to his dilemma, he felt that the best thing to do was to go ahead and flip a coin.

So, out comes a coin, he decides which option is going with which side, and as he stands on the mud at the side of the lake, he tosses the coin into the air.

Now, this sounds fair, as it would lead to one decision

winning over the other, but it didn't. Unfortunately for poor old Jeremiah, the coin landed on its edge in the mud meaning it had failed to land on either side.

For most people, they would either decide that this was a sign that killing themselves was a bad idea or do it again. However, he decided against doing either. So, what did he do instead? He went home and shot himself!

That's a Bit Rich

You have to admit that the IRS are pretty good at catching those individuals that do not complete their tax return, but it seems that some individuals just believe that the work they do somehow does not qualify.

Take the case of an exotic dancer as a prime example. She was busted by the IRS for not declaring her income, and you might think that there is nothing unusual in that.

However, it does become a bit strange when you consider that it was her income from just one guy. Apparently, she was paid over $1 million to have sex with the guy and failed to then declare her earnings. Somehow the IRS caught wind of all of this and busted her as a result.

Poor Mary

When it comes to popular names, it is hard to find anything that can surpass the popularity of Mary. Okay, so it might not be as popular in the world today as it was before, but that is because it would be tough to compete when you look at the success it had as the most popular name for a girl in the United States.

Up until 1947, Mary was the most popular name for a total of

67 consecutive years. Now, that is pretty impressive when you consider the competition that it was having to face up to on a yearly basis. For most of those years, it was streets ahead of anything else, even though we have no idea as to why this was the case, but in 1947 its run came to an end.

Oh, and the name that finally managed to take that top spot was—Linda.

Hands Up for the Dummy

Police officers are hardly known for their sense of humor, but that has not always been the case. Back in 1993, the police held a ballot to vote on a rather intriguing issue concerning a police officer by the name of Bob Geary.

Was the ballot to give him some award for an amazing moment of bravery? Was it to have him brought back into the police force after being suspended for having done something wrong?

Nope.

Instead, the ballot was to decide if he was going to be allowed to go on foot patrol while carrying a ventriloquist dummy. The surprising thing was that the ballot passed the motion, so off Bob went with his hand up the dummy who went by the name of Brendan O'Smarty.

Until he retired, both Officer Geary and Brendan became familiar faces as they patrolled the streets of San Francisco. However, you do wonder how on earth he would have been able to arrest someone when he had a dummy on his arm.

Do Shakespeare in its Real Voice

Whenever you read anything by Shakespeare, you would be perfectly normal if you thought that very little of it made sense. Often, you are forced into thinking very hard indeed about what was said and how it all pulls together into a play that actually means something.

However, it seems that there is one simple trick that you might want to employ the next time you venture towards reading something by the Bard himself.

According to Shakespeare experts, everything becomes so much easier to understand when you read it in the voice from the time when it was written. In other words, throw away your modern accent and way of reading things, and try to use the pronunciation that was more prevalent back in his time. Not only does it become easier to understand, but it is also meant to be funnier as well, which may very well be a deal-breaker for some people.

Stephen Hawking Keeps on Going

When it comes to a human being with an amazing mind, you have to admit that Stephen Hawking is right up there as being one of the greatest that has ever lived. Of course, his achievements take on even greater meaning when you remember that he has ALS.

But this is the one thing that is perhaps the most amazing thing in his life.

People that suffer from ALS do not generally live too long after they have received their diagnosis; it is just part of the disease. Step forward Stephen Hawking, because apart from being perhaps the most famous person alive today with the disease, he has also managed to live with it for over 50 years.

Now in his 70s, he was expected to die in his early twenties, so that is pretty remarkable.

Mountain Dew and Mice

Have you ever heard of an individual trying to sue a big-name company for something strange in the hope that they will get some money out of them? Well, you would find it difficult to find anything that is crazier than this case.

A man in the US attempted to sue Pepsi by stating that he found a mouse in his bottle of Mountain Dew. You might think that they would just settle out of court and offer him a small amount of money for it to go away but Pepsi had other ideas.

Ultimately, the man lost his court case and it was all thanks to Pepsi showing that his claims just were not possible.

To do this, they showed that a bottle of Mountain Dew would dissolve a mouse within 30 days. Yep, they actually did go ahead and prove that in a court of law. Furthermore, they also showed that the man had bought the bottle 74 days after it had been manufactured, so it was impossible for there to have been a mouse in his bottle.

You have to admit that this is pretty impressive, but at the same time it makes you wonder what may have been in the bottle that has now simply dissolved into the liquid.

What a Bright Spark

Lightning is pretty impressive to watch. The way in which those bolts either shoot across the sky or down to the ground is quite surreal. However, the one thing that you certainly never want to happen is to be caught outside when there is lightning around, as there is every chance that you could be unfortunate enough to be hit.

Now, being hit by lightning can kill, and for most people that will sadly be the case. Well, that is perhaps not entirely true if your name is Roy C. Sullivan.

Roy was a U.S Park Ranger who was certainly proud of his job. Of course, it meant being outside a lot of the time, so it would inevitably lead to him being in nature when a storm struck. For some, this would not be a problem, but it appears that Roy had an unfortunate ability to attract a storm and turn himself into a lightning conductor.

Yep, Roy was actually struck by lightning a staggering seven times and lived to tell the tale. This happened between 1942 and 1977, and considering the chances of being killed with one strike are pretty high, then to survive seven different occasions is just astonishing.

Do you think that Roy would glow in the dark after all of that?

Well, That's a Dead Cert

Horse racing has always had its ups and downs. Over the years, a number of horses have died along with various jockeys. However, back in 1923, something rather remarkable happened that has just never been repeated since.

The location was Belmont Park in New York, and the jockey in question for this piece of trivia was Frank Hayes.

By the end of his race, Frank was proclaimed the winner, but he was dead. It appears that during the race, poor Frank had a heart attack and died. Somehow, his body stayed on the saddle with him draped across the horse which continued on its path towards a glorious victory. The horse wasn't even expected to be challenging, as it was a 20-1 outsider, so there was certainly a double surprise when it crossed the finishing line first.

Now, that is what you call a dead cert.

Well, this is Unfriendly

Back in 2009, Burger King came up with a rather unusual marketing idea that certainly managed to obtain some publicity. Well aware of the impact that social media was having on the world, they decided to try to get in on the act in a unique way.

Their aim was to convince people to unfriend 10 people, and when they did this, they would then qualify for a free Whopper. Not only that, but the individuals who were then no longer your friends would be sent a message stating that their friendship was worth less than a Whopper to you.

For some, it was genius. For others it was crude and slightly unfair to individuals. However, it made the kind of mark that Burger King was looking for, although they have not repeated the stunt since then.

Twister isn't a Game

Any party that includes Twister as a game is going to be a winner. There is just something about us getting ourselves into strange positions, while trying not to fall over, that means hilarity will indeed ensue. Add in some alcohol, and you have the best party of all time.

However, it has not always been a favorite of everyone since it was released in 1966. Back then, the game did have its critics, but it was not because it hardly included the individual to show intelligence in any way. Instead, the critics claimed that it wasn't even a game and was merely sex in a box.

Yep, they actually said 'sex in a box' when describing Twister. Well, if that is how they saw it, then somebody better tell them that they were playing it wrong.

Imagine Terminator without Arnie

There are times when an actor is able to make a role their own to such an extent that you could never imagine somebody else playing that part. Stallone as Rocky, Ford as Indiana Jones, the list could go on and on, and included in that list is Arnie as the Terminator.

But then, it was a close-run thing for him to get the part to begin with as studio bosses had somebody else in mind. That individual was no other than O.J. Simpson.

So, why did they decided to go against this idea and give the role to Arnie instead? It seems that the bosses believed that nobody would be able to take O.J. Simpson seriously as a remorseless killer. That does come across as being a bit of a silly assumption to make considering now most people could easily see him as being a remorseless killer.

Now, That is Ambidextrous

People are quite settled on the idea that Leonardo da Vinci was a pretty impressive guy. To most, he was far ahead of his time and was a bit of a genius. However, it seems that he had another talent that was in its own right very impressive.

Apparently, da Vinci had the amazing ability to write with one hand and, at the same time, draw with the other. Of course, he would be pretty good at doing both things together and would be better at it than the majority of individuals, but go ahead and try to do it on your own. The chances are that one of the things will end up looking not even remotely close to anything that is able to be recognized.

Could You Believe there are Initials on the Moon?

The last man who was able to walk on the moon went by the name of Gene Cernan. He did so as part of the mission of Apollo 17 back in 1972. As he was the last individual to step off the moon, it was at that point that he was able to make this claim.

However, before he left on his mission, he promised is daughter that he would put her initials on the moon. You have to admit that this would be some pretty cool claim to fame, and it was a promise that Cernan was indeed able to keep.

The best part of all of this is simply the fact that thanks to the atmosphere on the moon, the initials TDC are more than likely going to remain there for tens of thousands of years. That is what you call a time capsule, and you wonder what people in the future will think when they stumble across it.

Do You Want Coffee in the Office?

According to a Professor of Microbiology at the University of Arizona, the coffee mugs in offices around the country may not be as healthy as you would like to think. However, it does go wayyyy further than anybody could ever imagine when you look at the reason as to why he believes that they are not healthy.

Studies conducted by the Professor have shown that 20% of office mugs that are used for coffee in the United States may come with a rather unwanted surprise. Something that is probably going to result in you only ever using your own mug or getting take-away.

What could be so bad to merit such a reaction?

Well, it is said that 20% of coffee mugs contain aspects of fecal matter in them. Yes, we did say fecal matter, and we apologize if you are at work drinking coffee as you read this.

Of course, we have to just guess as to how it gets there or why it seems to hang around, but it may very well make you think twice about drinking coffee in the office in the future.

Poor Kitty

Spies have constantly tried to find new ways to listen in on their enemy, and you have to admit that they can have some genius ideas that are able to give them an advantage. However, there are moments where they come up short and you wonder about the sanity of the individuals that are involved.

Take a 1960s plot by the CIA as a prime example. This was obviously in the middle of the Cold War, where trying to get any information on the Russians and inside the Kremlin was always going to be their number one priority. So, what did they come up with?

Rather surprisingly, they came up with the idea of using cats, but this was no normal approach to spying. Their aim was to implant an antenna, microphone, and batteries inside the cat in a program that was called Acoustic Kitty. Yes, there was an idea to turn a cat into a spying machine and then send it into the Kremlin or Russian Embassies to see what it could pick up.

Perhaps it does not come as a surprise to discover that the plan was a failure.

You Can Still Duel

The concept of having a duel to sort out your differences is something that we often believe to be in the past and during a time when this was really seen as being the manly way of sorting out an argument. In the civilized world, we like to think that those days are behind us and we have other methods that can be employed.

Well, that is true for everywhere other than Paraguay, where the idea of having a duel is still something that is allowed. There is no law against it, but there is one stipulation that both parties must stick to for it to then become a legal way of dealing with things.

So, what is this stipulation? Both parties have to be registered as a blood donor, so if one of them is indeed shot, then at least other people from elsewhere have the ability to benefit from it. Well, that does seem like a fair thing to ask.

Pointing the Direction

For a mountaineer, climbing Mt. Everest is the pinnacle of the sport in more ways than one. It is known to be dangerous, but the challenge is something that so many individuals feel that they have to tackle.

Of course, people know their way up the mountain, as it has been conquered on numerous occasions, but there are literally a few helping hands along the way to help you to keep on the correct path. So, what are these helping hands? Well, they are the corpses of some of the climbers that died on the mountain.

Over the years, hundreds of individuals have perished on Everest in a variety of ways, and not every corpse is able to then be brought down and given a proper burial. Instead, they are left there, and some of them are now used as markers to guide people up the mountain. It makes the mind boggle when you think of trying to describe the directions to someone there for the first time. 'So, you take a left past the skeleton guy with the black hat.'

Beer as a Soft Drink?

With alcohol, is there anything that is more famous than beer? It comes in all shapes and sizes as well as strengths and tastes, and everybody knows that drinking too much of it is going to lead to all kinds of problems for you.

But it hasn't always been like that, especially if you lived in Russia.

Rather surprisingly, the Russians only began to see beer as an alcoholic drink since 2011. Before that, it was classified as a soft drink along with the likes of Coke. It makes you wonder how on earth it could take so long for this decision to be made, but then if they don't see beer as being alcohol, how strong does something need to be before it can be classified as such?

Snow is Like Magic for Most

Snow is something that a number of us take for granted when we live in certain parts of the world. It is one of those things that we just know we are going to see every single year, and if we don't, it is a rare thing indeed.

However, a lot of people that encounter snow on a regular basis are unaware that they are in the minority rather than majority.

In fact, two-thirds of the population of the world have never seen snow with their own eyes. They can only go by images, whether that be photographs or video. Of course, they can still appreciate the coldness of it all, but apart from that, they have no idea what it is like to actually experience it in any way, shape, or form.

A Psycho Melon

When it comes to movies that sum up the thriller genre, it would be difficult to find anything that could beat *Psycho* for the way in which it can play on your mind. Of course, there are so many different scenes that stand out, but perhaps the key one has to be the infamous shower scene.

Anybody that has watched the movie will be able to remember it along with the terrifying sound effects, but if you knew how the sound effects were made, it could make things slightly less scary for you.

Keep in mind that the movie was made in 1960, so it was hardly a case of special effects being out of this world or sounds being added in digitally after it was shot. Nope, they had to go for something that was far more basic in its approach, and yet it was still something that worked.

In the shower scene, the sound effects were able to be created by repeatedly stabbing a casaba melon. Yep, it was achieved via a melon, and that is hardly something that you would expect to have been used.

A Different Olympic Games

The Olympic Games have been around for over a century, and during that time have included different sports that you would not even think were actually a sport. Some have only appeared once before then vanishing into oblivion, and one such example has to be the 1904 Olympics that were based in St. Louis.

Now, the games were not on the same scale as they are now, with fewer countries and substantially fewer competitors, but it is the actual events that we are more concerned about. At these games, you were able to represent your country in 3 events that just defy belief.

First, there was the pole climbing event. Yes, pole climbing. Next, there was rock throwing—and imagine trying to win a gold medal by throwing a rock. Finally, there was mud fighting, which has to win an award for the most bizarre event ever. Also, they would aim them at what were classed as 'tribal' people, and it's no surprise that the Olympic Games in 1904 ended up being a complete and utter disaster.

Don't Stop that Sneeze

Sneezing is annoying, and who on earth is happy about it happening? Clearly nobody is happy, but at the same time you should never try to suppress that sneeze just because the actual act of it annoys you so much.

Nope, you are advised to just allow it to happen because the act of suppressing it can end up being one of the worst decisions that you have ever made in your life. Why? By trying to stop that sneeze, you are going to be putting added pressure on blood vessels in both your head and neck, with the outcome being that you could end up rupturing one and, well, dying.

Yes, you could actually die from it, which is pretty scary when you stop and think about it for a moment.

Your Shoes Better Be Made for Walking

There are a few crazy stats connected to human beings that are always thrown up at random times. These stats are able to show you the kind of things that we get up to in our lives without even really being aware of it all.

So, what is the crazy stat at this point? Well, the title should perhaps give it away because this is all about walking.

According to some rather clever people that have thought about it, the average human being does enough walking during their life to have walked around the world three times. That is in itself pretty impressive, especially when you hardly feel as if you have done that as the total sneaks up on you on a daily basis.

Now, your shoes better be made for walking or there may be trouble ahead.

Can You Really Trust a Raisin?

Raisins are seen as being a healthy snack, but are they as healthy as you think? Of course, you could be sitting there wondering how on earth a raisin could be different, but that is until you look at various regulations as to what is allowed.

You need to remember where raisins come from, but even then, you would be hard-pressed to be able to imagine what is coming next. You see, according to the FDA, for every 8 ounces of raisins, there is allowed to be a maximum of 10 insects along with 35 eggs belonging to the fruit fly.

Yes, the regulations do allow for the inclusion of those very things, and that in itself is pretty unreal, and it may very well make you change your mind when faced with the prospect of eating some raisins.

Is it Me or am I Shorter?

As we get older, we also shrink. However, at this moment in time we are talking about something that does not happen over years or decades, but something that happens over and over again on a daily basis.

If you measure your height with absolute precision when you get out of bed and then do so again in the evening just before you go back to bed, you are going to notice a difference. For most people, the difference is around 1% of their height, and as you may have expected, it is all to do with the way in which we battle the weight of gravity against our spine.

As the day progresses, the spaces between joints, bones, and muscles are all getting smaller, and it is that movement that ultimately leads to us getting smaller.

That is a Big Yawn

Most people are aware that a hippo has a rather impressive yawn, but just how big is it on average? Well, thanks to the way in which their jaws operate, they can open up their mouths to a crazy angle, and coupled with the overall size of the hippo in general, it means that there is a pretty impressive mouth and space to fill.

As a result, some researchers have worked out that, on average, the space is large enough to accommodate a four-foot-tall child, which is pretty amazing when you stop and picture that for a moment.

Now, we just hope that they didn't try this out by using an actual child to check that they were correct in their assessment.

Somebody Give Him a Fright

Having the hiccups is annoying. It is one of those strange things that the body is able to do that gets on the nerves of every single human being when it strikes. However, we are all familiar with different potential remedies that are going to cure it, from drinking out of the wrong side of a cup to holding your breath, or giving someone a fright to effectively shock their body back into its normal way of working.

This all sounds pretty good, but spare a thought for poor old Charles Osbourne, who just could not get rid of his bout of hiccups no matter how hard he tried. In fact, this bout would go on and on with no sign of stopping, and he ended up having them for a grand total of 69 years.

Just think about that for a moment because that is longer than a lot of people are alive, and yet, he had to cope with having the hiccups! Perhaps his friends and family really had to improve their scaring someone approach as it was clearly not working in his case.

Do You Want to Breathe in the Subway?

So, you know that the subway is going to be a breeding ground for various bacteria and viruses. If you travel on there on a regular basis, then there is every possibility that you will pick up all kinds of illnesses, and it is often due to the air that you are breathing in.

However, even though we do seem to kind of accept that this is the case, it seems that a rather surprising percentage of the air is made up of something that you are probably going to feel a bit sick about when you think of it entering your body.

You see, it is believed that in a typical subway station that approximately 15% of the air content actually consists of particles of human skin. Now, just stop for a moment and imagine all of that coming into your mouth and then your lungs. Does that not make you want to stop what you are doing and reconsider how you are going to be breathing when you next venture into the subway?

Perhaps the Japanese had the correct idea when it came to wearing those masks.

Well, That's a Clean Giraffe

A giraffe is a pretty cool animal, and it is certainly different than anything else that you will have ever set eyes on in your life. However, its dimensions also mean that it has a number of rather cool party tricks under its sleeve that would be hard for any other animal to be able to beat.

Take its ears, for example. They are themselves pretty impressive, but they are just so high up, and it begs the question as to how on earth they are able to keep them clean. The answer to that is simply that the giraffe will lick them clean. Now, if you are wondering as to how it is able to do this, then keep in mind that it has an amazing 21-inch-long tongue.

Yes, 21 inches!

With a tongue that size, it's no wonder that it is able to do things such as clean out its ears, but we still would not fancy doing that with our own tongue, if we had that choice.

Pope John Paul II and Basketball

Pope John Paul II was famous for not only being the Pope, which is a good claim to fame, but also the fact that he was a goalkeeper for a soccer team before he became a priest. However, perhaps sport was kind of in his blood, a theory which is backed up by an event that happened in the year 2000.

It was in that year that Pope John Paul II was named an honorary Harlem Globetrotter. Now, he clearly had no intention of playing or anything of the sort, but it seems that he was still more than happy to accept the award as it is surely the dream of so many people around the world to be on that team?

You have to admit, it would have been pretty cool if he had appeared for them.

Fortune Cookies aren't Chinese

There is something distinctly Chinese about the idea of fortune cookies, but there is a problem, and it is quite a big one. The problem is that the fortune cookie concept is not even Chinese in origin. Instead, it seems that it was an American that was able to come up with the idea almost a century ago, and it has gone from strength to strength since then.

The man in question went by the name of Charles Jung, and back in 1918, he decided to create the fortune cookie just to add some fun to an evening. People loved getting those sayings appearing in their food, so the idea was quick to take off. Over the decades, the concept of the fortune cookie spread high and wide throughout the country, with it eventually becoming the phenomenon that we know today.

That Flea is for the High Jump

People are generally aware that a flea is pretty good at jumping. However, you may not be aware of just how good they are or how you could compare it to what you yourself are able to do from a jumping point of view.

It has been worked out that the flea can jump a staggering 350 times its body length, which is just an insane figure to try to comprehend. In order to put it into perspective, a human being would need to comfortably jump the length of a football field to achieve the same thing.

Considering a long jumper cannot jump over 9m, it just lets you see that we can never achieve this remarkable feat.

If Only the Names Had Stayed

There are times when places are going to change their name, or there are at least other ideas as to what they would be called. However, most individuals will be blissfully unaware that the place where they reside was initially intended to be called something else.

Take these three states as prime examples.

Tennessee is, of course, famous for a number of things, but it wasn't always known by that name. Instead, it was previously known as Franklin, which just doesn't seem to have the same ring to it.

There is also West Virginia, which may have always been known by that name, but that's not to say that there weren't ideas to refer to it as something else. In fact, it was initially to be called Kanawha before the West Virginia idea came to fruition.

Finally, there is Utah. It was apparently very close to becoming known as Deseret.

Watch Out for the Deadly Coconuts

We know that sharks are deadly, but to be honest, there are not that many people that die as a result of a shark attack each year. This surprises a lot of people, and to show how rare it is we can compare it to the number of deaths caused by other things that we just never view as being so dangerous.

Take this as a good example. On a yearly basis, there are more people killed by falling coconuts than shark attacks. Just think about that for a second. If you are in an area where there are coconuts, then perhaps you shouldn't be thinking too much about the dangers in the sea; it's more about the dangers above you that should be concerning to you.

What are the Chances?

Something such as playing the lottery is clearly a game of chance. You select your numbers and then wait to see if you are lucky enough for them to be selected. Most people are even aware that the chances of them winning are stacked against them, but it can be useful to put it into some kind of perspective.

For example, do you know that there is a greater chance of you actually being killed on your way to pay for your lottery entry than the chances of you winning the jackpot? To be honest, you are also more likely to die from being left-handed and using a right-handed item incorrectly than winning the lottery.

The list goes on and on when compared to some lotteries where the chances of winning are in the region of 1 to 170 million. You are even more likely to win an Academy Award than the lottery, and yet we still try our best even though we have very little chances of being successful.

So, maybe think about the chances before you go and spend all of that cash.

Your Eyes

You will obviously be familiar with the fact that human beings grow physically from the moment we are born. Even after we stop growing in height, our ears and nose continue to just keep on going until the day we die.

However, it's not all like that in our body.

You would expect that, as we get bigger, we need everything in our body to increase in size as we develop and, for the most part, that is true. The only part of the body where that doesn't apply is our eyes because, rather surprisingly, they stay the same size from the moment we are born.

So, when you next see a baby and are amazed at the size of its eyes staring back at you, just remember that they are not going to get any bigger. It is just down to our head getting bigger that it appears as if our eyes adjust accordingly.

And You Sleep on it

A good mattress is often hard to come by, and it partly explains why we tend to hang onto one that provides us with a great sleep for as long as possible. However, this is not always a good idea, especially when you discover one rather disturbing fact about it all.

You see, apart from the fact that we are supposed to change our mattress after a number of years due to the lost support, there is a whole lot more to it than that. According to research, the average mattress ends up doing something peculiar if you have been using it for a decade.

So, what is that peculiar thing that will make you change your mind about your mattress?

On average, it is going to double in its weight over the course of a decade and it is all connected to the buildup of dust mites and their poop. Yep, all of that is underneath you as you dream away blissfully unaware of what you are lying on.

Do you think that you will now go out and purchase a new mattress?

Colonial Africa

If you check out the history of Africa, then you will see how it was effectively divided up by different countries that were seeking to create their Empire. The British, French, Portuguese, Belgians, the list goes on and it takes away from a rather startling fact about Africa that has long been forgotten.

Before the Colonial forces appeared on the continent, it is believed that Africa consisted of a staggering 10,000 different states. Inside the states were autonomous groups, and they had their very own culture and language. Of course, the idea of colonization took all of that away as groups were forced to live together and their history was disrupted.

So, the next time you look at the map of Africa, just imagine how different it could have been if things had been left alone.

I Can See but Can't Think

An ostrich is a big bird. However, it seems that size is not always going to be everything. In fact, the ostrich has a rather unfortunate size problem that is having a detrimental impact on its ability to have a better life.

You see, while you may be impressed with the size of its wings, body and legs, or even its neck, if you look deep inside, you will not be as impressed with other parts. The reason for this is because the brain of an ostrich is smaller in size than its eyes which, by all accounts, makes this a pretty dumb animal.

Perhaps that is the reason why it cannot fly—simply because it doesn't have the brain power to work it out on its own?

Heroin Used to be Trademarked

There is little doubt that heroin has been a drug that has caused a huge amount of misery around the world. It then makes it even more remarkable to learn that the term 'heroin' used to be trademarked, and it was one of the largest pharmaceutical companies in the world that owned it.

In the early 1900s, and going back further in time, the trademark was held by the company Bayer. They actually lost aspects of the trademark after the end of WWI simply because they were a German company and it was part of the Treaty of Versailles.

They used to sell it in bottles as a cure for various ailments until it was better understood regarding the way in which it was so addictive and difficult to stop taking. You might also want to know that, for a time at least, it was sold as a potential cure for a cough!

We need to stress that we are talking about the laboratory version, but then it's not really any different to the drug that people abuse since it all derives from a morphine base.

That's a Lot of Bites

People know that a mosquito is going to land on your skin and get some blood. However, have you ever wondered about how many of those annoying flying insects it would take for the entire human body to be drained of blood? Nope? Well, we are going to tell you anyway.

It's pretty cool to think that somebody has worked this out, but we know the average amount of blood a single mosquito can take at any given time as well as the average amount of blood that a human being has in their body. By knowing these things, we can work out that it would take 1.2 million of them to achieve this particular feat.

Now, you have to admit that this is a lot of bites on your body, but the next time you see a mosquito, just remember that he is not going to be able to get a lot out of you, unless he has a number of friends behind him.

Watch Out when Left-Handed

The majority of people are right-handed, but spare a thought for those individuals that prefer to use their left hand for different actions. If you look around, a number of items are designed purely for individuals that are right-handed, and that causes a problem if you are not that way inclined.

However, you might be amazed to hear just how big a problem this can cause for left-handed individuals.

According to statistics, each year sees somewhere in the region of 2,500 people dying as a result of being left-handed and trying to use an item that is designed for someone who is right-handed. In other words, they are trying to do it with their weaker hand, putting them in danger, but then nobody would ever dare to dream that they could die as a result?

So, if you are left-handed for anything at all, just keep this fact in mind because it could end up being a pretty good decision to leave an action to someone else.

How Fast to Become a Millionaire?

Everybody would love to be a millionaire, unless you already are one, but do you know how long it could take you to reach that all-important milestone? Well, chances are that it will not take as long as you had perhaps thought.

The only problem is that it does involve just a single method which, on the face of it, sounds pretty easy to do although that is not always the case.

So, what is this method that we speak of? Well, let's say you start off with $0.01 to your name. It sounds as if it would take you forever to become rich, but that's not the case.

Instead, if you merely doubled your money every single day, it would only take a total of 27 days for you to ultimately become a millionaire. Now, that is pretty impressive, so what are you waiting for?

How to Understand Statues Involving a Horse

There are more than enough examples of statues where the individual is on a horse, but do you know what they actually mean? Delve deeper into it and you will find that there are different ideas being employed and that the statue itself is able to tell us more about the individual than you perhaps expected.

Look at the horse in particular. If the horse has both front legs in the air, then it means the person on the horse died in battle. If one leg is on the ground, then they eventually died from injuries that were initially sustained on the battlefield. If both front legs are on the ground, then they eventually died from natural causes.

Of course, you then have to look closer at the inscription that accompanies the statue to determine when they died and the battle they were involved in, but just by studying the horse, you at least have an idea what to expect.

That is a Long Tapeworm

The idea of a tapeworm being in the human body is not exactly a pleasant thing to consider. However, this entire scenario gets worse when you then discover the facts about the longest one that has ever been uncovered within the human body.

The exact details of who had it are difficult to ascertain, but doctors reported that one individual who was complaining of being unwell actually had a tapeworm inside their body that measured a staggering 33m. For others, that is over 108ft of tapeworm, which makes you wonder how on earth their body was able to operate and do anything at all.

Now, just imagine trying to pass that kind of thing all on your own. How numb would your legs get just from sitting there?

That is a Heavy Gut

Your gut is a hive of activity, but most people are unaware of just how busy it is down there even when you are not having anything to eat or drink.

On average, your gut contains over 400 different strains of bacteria, but thankfully, most of them are good guys. However, all of this bacteria generally weighs in the region of 3 pounds, which is in itself pretty impressive.

The scary part is that if your body failed with its natural protection, the bacteria in your gut would end up completely consuming you in next to no time. Actually, it would effectively eat you from the inside out and do so within 48 hours of your body halting its natural job.

Pubic Hair Causes Damage

Pubic hair, you either love it or your hate it, but if you work in sewage then you are going to absolutely loathe it. Why? Well, we need to look more closely at what it can do, and you will probably look at your pubes in a completely different light.

We all know that our sewage works has to deal with some rather disgusting things that will clog up the pipes, but even though you may have your own ideas as to what could cause the most damage, the truth is somewhat closer to home.

Yep, you have probably already guessed the direction that this is heading in, but the one thing that is able to really block the drains unlike pretty much anything else is pubic hair. Not only that, but it is pretty tough for them to handle, and it is all to do with the fact that it is not only insoluble but will also get through the vast majority of filtration systems.

Ultimately, vast quantities of pubic hair are removed from the sewage system every single month or they run the very real risk of the entire system becoming blocked. Perhaps it's best not to flush it down the toilet in the future because think of those poor workers that then need to deal with it further down the line.

Sticky Chewing Gum?

When you were a kid and given gum to chew, there is a pretty good chance that your mother told you not to swallow it or else it would stick to your intestines for a number of years. This was enough to scare a number of children into never wanting to chew it, and for those that did there would be years of mental torture to follow.

But what's the truth? Can it stick to your intestines in the way that your mother described?

The quick answer is that no it can't. In fact, it will just pass through your system without any problems whatsoever and you will end up depositing it in just the same way as other food that you have been eating recently.

But that's not to say that it will always be like this. For reasons that are unknown, there have been some incidents where it did not become as plain sailing as it should be.

Instead, some rather unlucky people have found that the gum has become stuck to their rectum, and your mind is probably working overtime as to how horrible this would be to fix. It ended up with them developing one or two issues when passing long, sticky pieces of gum.

What a Fart Bubble

People generally know that the blue whale is a massive animal, and it seems that it is capable of being huge in pretty much every department.

Take the way in which it farts as a prime example. Now, you would rightfully expect that an animal of this size would produce a fart that was equally as impressive, but you will probably be taken aback by just how big it ends up being.

As it is in water, the blue whale produces a fart bubble, and the shocking thing is that the fart bubble it can produce is large enough that it could accommodate a horse. Just imagine what us humans would be like if we were able to produce something that was as equally impressive as that, but then the world would be a very smelly place indeed.

We Shed a Lot

If you were of the opinion that it was just snakes that shed their skin, then think again. Instead, we humans are right up there with the best when it comes to getting rid of our skin, as it is believed that the human being will completely change the outer layer of their skin every second month.

In order to achieve this, we have to shed in the region of 40 pounds of skin, and you can just imagine where all of that ends up going on a daily basis. Also, this is something that we continue to do throughout our lives, so you have a lot of shedding to do and a lot of new skin to grow before your time is up.

Is Sherlock Holmes Real?

When it comes to fictional detectives, it would be difficult to find one that has had as big an impact as Sherlock Holmes. In fact, it seems that his ability to capture the imagination of the public has been taken to a whole new level, according to a survey from the United Kingdom in 2008.

In the survey, teenagers in the country were quizzed on a series of famous figures, some real and others fictional. Rather surprisingly, 58% of teenagers that were quizzed actually believed that Sherlock Holmes was a real individual, and just to make matters worse, a rather staggering 20% thought that Winston Churchill was fake.

When you see stats such as that, it does make you wonder about some people, especially when you consider the famous figures that were involved.

The Irish Population and the Potato Famine

The potato famine of Ireland was an absolute turning point in the history of the country. Occurring in 1845 and lasting until 1852, disease destroyed the potato crop, which lead to a huge number of individuals leaving the country to avoid the risk of starving to death.

However, the surprising thing is the population of the country and the fact that it has still not recovered to the same level it was before the potato famine, which happened all of those years ago.

Before the famine, it is believed that the population of the country was in the region of anywhere between 8.5 million and 9 million. In 2017, the population of Ireland is still only approximately 4.5 million, even though it has increased in the last century. This just shows the impact that the famine had on the country, and it is still something that it has never really recovered from, at least from a population point of view.

The Great Pacific Garbage Patch

A lot of garbage ends up getting into the oceans, but you are probably not aware of just how much is thrown out and never picked up. Of course, when you have an area the size of the Pacific, nothing is going to be small, as a lot of countries border it, but even taking that into consideration does not accurately explain the sheer size of what is known as the Great Pacific Garbage Patch.

Through observations, it is believed that this garbage patch actually covers the same area size as the state of Texas. This means it covers approximately 270,000 square miles, and as you can imagine that is a lot of garbage. Of course, this garbage patch includes so many different items from various countries that it is impossible to accurately take stock, but just imagine what that is doing and how this garbage dump has now gotten out of control.

Are You Related to Genghis Khan?

When it comes to ancient feared warlords, Genghis Khan has to be right up there as being one of the names that would appear on your list. But what are your chances of being related to him?

Surprisingly enough, the chances are about 1 in 200, and it is all to do with the appearance of a particular chromosome in the population. Okay, so this is actually a bit of a stretch, as we are primarily talking about Asia, but it still works out at 0.5% of the total population of the world.

With this, we are talking about a Y-Chromosome that has been traced back in its lineage to the area of Genghis Khan over 1000 years ago. Also, his body has never been found, so we don't know for certain if it is linked directly to him, but it is still something pretty cool to tell the grandchildren.

Twins Born Days Apart?

When you think of twins, you expect that one follows the other in being born just a matter of minutes later. Of course, you might say that it takes an hour or perhaps two at the most. If you discover that twins are born on different days, then you simply think that they were born either side of midnight and it doesn't confuse the mind.

But in 2012, something completely different happened in the UK.

A couple were celebrating the fact that they were going to have twins when the mother went into labor early, four months early to be more precise. As a result, one twin was born premature even though she was told that there was a very good chance that both would die.

As it turned out, the other twin decided that it was not time for her to make an appearance to the world just yet, so while her twin sister fought for her life in a special baby unit, she stayed there quite content.

It was not until after 36 weeks that the doctors decided that it was safe to induce the pregnancy so she could give birth to the second twin, but if nature had been left to take its course, the record would be even longer.

At the end of the day, there was a total of 87 days between the births of the twins, setting a new record that had stood since the 1990s.

Pac-Man and Pizza

When it comes to a legendary game, then you would be hard-pressed to be able to beat Pac-Man. However, have you ever thought about where the shape of the main character comes from?

Well, there is a story that claims to explain it all, and when you think about the shape then it seems to make a lot of sense.

When it was created, it is believed that the person behind the character, who went by the name of Tohru Iwantani, got his inspiration from a pizza. When you think about it, the character does indeed look like a pizza that has had a slice taken out of it, so it does all make sense.

So, the next time you take a slice, just pay homage to a classic video game at the same time.

Humans and Bananas

Let's face it, who in the world does not like bananas? However, perhaps you will change your mind a bit when you discover this rather interesting piece of trivia about the famous fruit.

Scientists have discovered that, rather surprisingly, we humans share about 50% of our DNA with a banana. Yep, you could technically say that we are either half banana or a banana is half human.

Of course, the way in which this works is all trapped in the intricacies of science, but there are more than enough reports out there that back up this claim. Also, does it not make you want to find out more about other fruits or vegetables that we could end up being related to?

A Plague of Dancing?

If we are honest, history has a habit of throwing up some rather strange events that we often then wonder as to whether they are true. Well, even though one event from 1518 in Strasbourg sounds bizarre, it is also very well documented that it did indeed occur.

So, what is this strange event that we are talking about? Well, it's a plague of dancing.

Back in 1518, it seems that people danced for a month in total, with some dancing non-stop for days on end. It is believed that around 400 people were involved, with it all beginning when a single woman started to dance manically in the street. Even though people were exhausted, they would continue dancing, with a number of them dying as a result of a whole host of different ailments.

71

Exactly why it happened is not known, but it is suspected that it could have been linked to a toxic chemical that would tend to develop on the type of wheat that was eaten in the area. However, that in itself is just a theory—compared to us knowing that this plague of dancing did indeed happen.

Why Airplane Food Isn't So Good

Whenever you are on a flight, do you end up feeling rather let down by the quality of the food that is offered? Well, if you do then you are certainly not alone, but it may be the case that it is due to something other than the companies employing the most horrible cooks to ever walk the face of the earth.

Instead, it may be better explained as being linked to the way in which the altitude and pressure inside the plane itself could be impacting our senses. In fact, it is believed that our sense of smell in particular is going to decrease by anywhere between 20% and 40%, and when you consider the role that smell plays in how we taste something, that will make a huge difference.

So, the next time you are on a flight and are offered something to eat, don't turn your nose up at it because it is more than likely going to be your own nose that is the problem.

Graffiti is Older than You Think

For many people, the idea of graffiti is a modern-day issue that ends up leaving a blight on the landscape. However, the act of adding some strange words or phrase to a piece of public property is older than you may think.

Some of the earliest examples of graffiti date back 2000 years and can still be seen even today. To do so, you need to go to Pompeii in Italy, and if you pay close attention to the walls of the buildings that still stand, then you will see some ancient graffiti that certainly has a different appeal than the modern equivalent.

Aside from people writing the almost customary note telling others that they were there, you will also find graffiti that is from a wife saying that she is not going to sell her husband. Now, that is not the kind of thing that you would see today, so perhaps ancient graffiti was far more advanced, at least in thought, than what we are now capable of.

Fergie was Sally

If you were a kid of the 80s, you more than likely watched Snoopy. In the show, you may also remember a character that went by the name of Sally. Well, did you ever wonder about any cartoon as to who the person was behind the voice?

If this does sound like you, then life becomes a bit easier when you look at who was behind the voice of Sally, as it was actually Fergie from the Black Eyed Peas. Yes, you are indeed thinking of the very same Fergie, and the idea of her being this voice is certainly going to confuse a number of people. However, you just need to remember that she was only a kid at the time, so perhaps she should be given a break.

How Much is that Art?

Everybody knows that art can be expensive, but you tend to get something for your money that you can then go ahead and admire. However, it is not always the case, which is crazy when you think about the money that can indeed be spent on it.

Take the case of a work of art that was purchased for $10,000 in 2011. Now, for some that may not even be a lot of money, but it suddenly sounds as if you have been conned when you discover what was purchased with that cash.

A woman by the name of Aimee Davison purchased a piece of art that went by the name of 'Fresh Air, so you can perhaps already identify the direction in which this is heading. It really was a piece of art that had nothing in it at all and was just an empty frame.

You would expect that Ms. Davison would be upset at this, but she actually knew what she was doing. It was her belief that in purchasing it, she would have a wing of the museum named after her, so even though she did indeed buy a piece of art that had nothing in it, she certainly benefited in other ways.

Land the Plane Now

There are a whole host of reasons as to why there may be an emergency landing of a flight. However, not all of them are as serious as you may have initially feared because there are moments where it is human error that is to blame rather than any technical issues.

Take a flight back in 2016 as a prime example. There was an attempt by an individual on the flight to make a complaint regarding the conduct of another individual. This flight in the US had the potential to take a bad turn if, in their opinion, something was not done.

But what could have incensed the individual so much that they had to go ahead and pass a handwritten note to a member of the staff? Of course, you may have expected it to involve some kind of terrorist threat and the silent note was so as not to draw attention, but that is not the case.

Instead, the note mentioned how they wanted the staff to deal with an individual sitting some 10 to 12 rows in front of them. Their crime? Having the most horrific smelling farts that they had ever experienced. Yep, they wanted the plane to pretty much turn around so that this individual could be removed from the plane thanks to their flatulence. Nothing was done about it, so you kind of hope that they filled the plane with their stench for its entire duration.

Eating from the Toilet

The concept of eating from the toilet is hardly one that you would want to entertain, but in Taiwan this is something that you can actually choose to do. Okay, it's not as bad as it sounds, which is confusing for most people as the mere thought is enough to put you off your food.

Instead, a restaurant serves its food on a miniature toilet just to be different and stand out from the crowd. It does take a bit of getting used to at first, and if you check out some images, you will see what we mean.

But then, 'Modern Toilet' does take things one step further with its bathroom inspired décor. For seats, you sit on toilets—but they are cushioned, so that is fine—and there are often bathtubs covered over for tables, so it is quite a unique setting. The restaurant seems to be doing quite well as they do have several chains—probably toilet chains—across the country, so people don't seem to be put off with the idea.

What's the Time in Las Vegas?

If you venture to Las Vegas, it makes sense that you will end up in a casino at some point. After all, this is part of the entire experience, and you could hardly go to the city and not check out something that is such a core part of its culture.

However, if you do go into a casino, make sure that you are wearing your watch. The reason is that there is a tendency for there to never be any clocks in the casinos, and that is a blatant attempt to get gamblers to forget about the passage of time and just lose themselves in the games. People get nervous when they are clock watching, so that is just not possible, and there are countless examples of individuals missing out on other things as they suddenly discover that they have spent hours in a casino.

So, just remember that it might not only be money that you lose but also time as well.

Where Did the Island Go?

Global warming has caused a number of problems around the world, but it has amazingly been linked to resolving an issue that existed between two countries.

The countries in question were India and Bangladesh, and the dispute was over land. So, how did global warming manage to make a difference? Well, the land in question was New Moore, and it was an island. Both countries claimed control of it, as it pretty much sat between them. However, this all changed in 2010 as the island simply vanished beneath the waves, so if there was no land left, then there could be no dispute.

Now, if only other global disputes could be resolved in this manner.

It's Nippy on Christmas Island

Christmas Island is not very well named when you consider that it is in the Indian Ocean. It is hardly going to create an image in your mind of the traditional Christmas complete with snow and children having snowball fights.

However, it is not its incorrect name that we are focusing on here, as our attention is directed toward a rather strange and wonderful natural event that occurs on the shores of this island on a yearly basis.

This event involves crabs, but not just one or two, as this is more akin to a sea of crabs invading the island. Of course, it is quite freaky to imagine this happening, but what makes it worse is that we are actually talking about millions of crabs at one time.

So, why are they doing this? Well, it's all about their mating, and they seem to converge on this island in order to seek out their mate and do what crabs do. It just so happens that they all seem to be in the mood at the same time resulting in it becoming more like Crab Island rather than Christmas Island. Furthermore, it is estimated that there may be up to 43 million crabs around the island during this period, so you'd better be careful where you stand.

Don't Venture to Snake Island

A lot of people fear snakes, and it is easy to understand why so you would hardly want to venture to a place that is known by the moniker 'Snake Island' as that would be insane on your part. The island itself is close to Sao Paulo in Brazil, and it is rather easy to see why it has been given this name when you check out a few statistics.

The island itself only covers a total of 110 acres, and yet a study has revealed that there are over 4000 snakes on this one single island. That works out to there being the equivalent of a snake every 6 square yards, and that does mean that you are going to come across them no matter where you go. If that is not scary enough, the island is also home to a snake that goes by the name 'Golden Lancehead' and even though it may look quite cool with its yellowish color, looks can be deceptive.

If you are unfortunate enough to be bitten by this snake, then there is a chance that your skin is going to start to melt, which has to be one of the scariest things that you could ever imagine happening to you.

That is a Big Family

If you are from a family that has just a couple of children, then you could hardly say that it was a big family. However, the same cannot be said for a family in India, as they can legitimately lay claim to being the biggest family in the world.

Now, you might be sitting there thinking that perhaps a husband and wife have 15 children or something along those lines to qualify, but it is much bigger than you could ever imagine.

The man in question goes by the name of Ziona Chana, and he lives in the Indian state Mizoram. Rather amazingly, he has 94 children, but then he does have 39 wives, which partly explains it. But then, it does get even bigger, as some of his children now have their own children and they live in the same home, so you can add to the number 14 in-laws as well as 33 grandchildren.

The entire family lives in a 100-room home which covers four stories. Apparently, they all work together to keep things running as smoothly as possible, but then with so many people under the one roof you can understand why it could hardly be left to just one or two individuals.

A Kangaroo Looks Happy

If you think of a kangaroo, what comes to mind? The chances are that you will think of them hopping along or with their babies in their pouch, and that is all pretty accurate and reasonable to consider.

However, there is one fact that a lot of people do not know about the kangaroo, which could very well change the way that you look at them. That fact is to do with part of their biology, and it is different from anything else that you will be able to find in the animal kingdom.

So, what is this fact?

Well, did you know that a female kangaroo has three vaginas? Yep, not just one but three of them. That is in itself pretty amazing, and it does make you wonder as to the reasons why, but who are we to judge them. They were clearly supposed to be made that way, so perhaps we should just leave them in peace because they will just box us if we corner them.

Would You Like Some Cheese?

There are thousands of different types of cheese around the world, and they are all able to cater to different tastes. However, there is one cheese in the world that is truly different from anything else that you would ever even dare to think about.

For this rather special cheese, we need to head on over to the Italian island of Sardinia. Of course, parts of Italy are pretty well known for their cheese, but in this instance, we are focusing on something called casa marzu.

Now, the name itself doesn't sound too bad at all, but it is what is contained within the cheese that is going to prove to be the scary part. This cheese has one secret ingredient that is not even that secretive when you eat it because stuck in the cheese are live maggots.

Yes, there are actual maggots in the cheese, and they are supposed to be there. If the thought of that is not bad enough for you, then perhaps this second point is going to prove to be too much.

The maggots will make their way out of the cheese as you eat it, or you hope that they do, but they have been known to leap out of the cheese to around five inches in height. Just imagine that for a moment where you are trying to enjoy the flavor only to then see a maggot flying towards your face.

So, would you like some cheese?

That's More Than Just a Step

Every man and his dog know that Neil Armstrong was the first man to set foot on the moon. A lot of people are also aware that Buzz Aldrin joined him soon after.

But then, even though Armstrong could take all of the accolades, it seems that good old Buzz was able to still become the first individual to do something on the moon— even though it may not have been what he had expected to do when approaching the moon.

It is believed that Buzz Aldrin became the first human being to have a pee on the moon. He did this almost as soon as he set foot on the surface of the moon, but clearly, he did it in his spacesuit rather than in the conventional manner. Even so, you have to admit that it is a pretty cool claim to fame.

The Village with No Roads

How would you like to live in a village where there are no roads? Of course, you will probably be imagining roads in the normal sense and then believing that there would be dirt roads or something else to replace them, but that is not the case.

To get a better understanding, we can look at a village in the Netherlands by the name of Giethoorn because this place is going to be pretty unique.

The village is picturesque, but the way in which the different homes are linked together is completely different to what you may expect to see. Instead of roads, the homes are linked together via a series of canals and footbridges, so there are no cars at all in the village. Of course, people can still arrive in their car, but they are left on the outskirts of the village free to walk around as they please.

Imagine Having Blue Skin

We are all familiar with the varieties of skin color that are in the world, but what about blue? You have probably never thought about people having blue skin, and you would imagine that it would be something out of a horror movie, but it's not.

You see, there was one family based in Kentucky that did indeed have blue skin, and you can imagine the looks that they would get whenever they were out and about. The family was known as the Fulgates of Troublesome Creek, and even though we are not absolutely certain as to how they managed to get their blue skin, we can guess.

According to the experts, it may have been as a direct result of a combination of two things. First, there may be an aspect of inbreeding within the family that could have contributed, but at the same time they were perhaps all suffering from a condition known as methemoglobinemia which is known to affect our genes. Put the two together, and it is just possible that it could very well lead to them developing blue skin.

The Red Ice

Ice is frozen water, we all know that. However, have you ever thought about the possibility of there being some red water that comes from ice? Nope? Well, that's understandable.

However, you will probably be surprised to hear that this is something that has actually happened. In order to find this rather strange event, we have to head to Antarctica, which is only really famous for penguins and a lot of ice. In Antarctica, there is a glacier that goes by the name 'blood falls' and it is pretty easy to guess why it has been given that title.

If you are fortunate enough to catch a glimpse of it at the correct time, you would see that the water that comes out of it is red in color. In fact, it makes it look as if the ice itself is bleeding.

Now, clearly that is not possible, but the water is indeed red, and it is all thanks to the water being oxidized. In other words, it is completely natural, and it is simply just a strange thing for you to come across.

Cross-Border Opera

You will find that there are people all around the world that enjoy watching opera, but an opera house in North America has something that is just a little bit different to any other venue that you may visit in order to see it being performed.

The reason why it is different is simply because the opera house sits on the border between the United States and Canada, but it goes further than that. In fact, what you will find with this opera house is that the stage is in one country and the audience sits in a completely different country, even though they are in the same building.

You have to admit that this is going to be a pretty unique setting for a performance of opera.

Well, That's a Different Toothpaste

A number of people are curious about the past and the way in which our ancestors handled certain things that we now take for granted. One major area that is often up for debate is surrounding the concept of personal hygiene, and it is clear that things were handled differently when you go back in time.

Take the Romans as an example. For their time, they were pretty well advanced when it came to hygiene, but they did take things to an absolute extreme in their quest to feel good. For example, you might be wondering how on earth they would brush their teeth, and what did they use for toothpaste?

Now, a number of cultures would use charcoal, and that is something that can still work today, but the Romans believed in something else. What they did was they would use urine to clean their teeth, and they do say that it works very well indeed. However, you might just have to take our word for it because you hardly want to go ahead and try that out now, or do you?

A Gecko is the Real Spiderman

So, this may sound like a contradiction in terms, but it seems that the gecko is pretty much the best animal version of Spiderman. Most people are aware that it is a pretty impressive climber, but it seems the gecko has a number of things helping it out.

To better understand things, we need to look more closely at their feet, and what we would find is that they have thousands of small hairs all over the surface, and those hairs are going to play a major role in helping them to climb and generally just hang around.

The key is that there is a chemical between the hairs, and it means that they effectively stick to surfaces which allows them to climb and just sit there. It also means that they can hang onto something with just a single toe and still not fear falling off, which you have to admit is pretty impressive.

A Long Time to Hold Your Breath

We humans are generally not that good at holding our breath, and we are certainly nowhere near as good as some of our animal world relatives. Take the Nile crocodile as a prime example. They are not only experts at catching their prey, but it seems that they have a huge amount of patience at the same time.

It is known that this form of crocodile has the ability to sit underneath the surface of the water and hold its breath for two hours at a time while it is waiting for its prey. That is seriously impressive, and it just makes you think about what is indeed lurking beneath the water should you ever find yourself looking at the Nile. Other crocodiles are just as good, so even if it looks all peaceful on the surface, it may be a completely different story underneath.

Kiss My Donkey

You may be familiar with some old wives' tales that are supposed to act as amazing remedies and capable of curing a wide range of ailments. While some of them are rooted in fact and can potentially work, there are some out there that are just crazy and make you fear for the sanity of the public that believe in them.

Take a treatment for toothache that was pretty widely believed back in the Middle Ages in Germany. It was their belief that you could go ahead and cure a toothache by kissing a donkey. Yep, giving a donkey a peck on its lips could somehow take away the pain that you felt from the toothache.

Of course, this is impossible, but it does then make you wonder about the theory that supported this idea to begin with. One potential answer is that it was hoped the donkey would be so thrown by the kiss that it would kick the individual in the face and knock the tooth out. To be honest, this is quite an extreme way of trying to deal with a toothache, and it is certainly not recommended.

Your Perfect Nap Time

If you are honest with yourself, then there is a pretty good chance that you will admit to enjoying a nap. However, scientists have been able to work out the best time for us to go and have a short sleep as it is directly tied into our body clock and also something quite natural that happens to us.

They say that the best time for us to have a nap is between

1pm and 2:30pm, and that it has nothing to do with the length of time we have been awake by the time we get to that 90 minutes. Instead, the scientists argue that our body temperature takes a slight drop at those times, even though it is completely natural, and that drop in our body temperature makes us feel sleepy. Of course, it does then rise again quite quickly, but if you are feeling slightly drowsy and tired around that time, at least you now know the reason why.

Corn is the Global Product

Produce that is grown in the world has a tendency to be found more in certain areas than others. This is entirely to do with the way in which they all require specific conditions in which to grow, and it is often difficult for each part of the world to be able to provide everything that a crop needs.

However, that is not entirely true, as there is one crop in particular that is perhaps able to be viewed as a global product, and it may not be what you expect.

The crop in question is corn, and it is able to be grown on every single continent with the exception of Antarctica, which is pretty easy to understand the reasons why, and it is certainly in abundance in each and every continent. Of course, there are different varieties that may only grow in certain areas, but at least some form of corn is able to be grown in pretty much every single country in the world, which is pretty impressive when you stop and think about it.

That Fruit Looks Like an Ant

When you think of fruit, there is a pretty good chance that you can imagine the shape of a number of different varieties. Of course, you are also aware that fruit does indeed vary in size, but few people know that fruit can be reduced in size to something that is pretty much non-existent.

The smallest fruit in the world is the utricle, and you would be forgiven for never having heard of this before as it is hardly the kind of thing that you see on the shelves in your local grocery store. In fact, the utricle is something that almost nobody has heard of.

Think of a strawberry and the small seeds that are on the side. They are actually small fruits with the seeds, and even though they are referred to as an achene on a strawberry, a utricle is pretty much the same thing.

So, why do we say that it looks like an ant? Well, there's no need to worry, as it doesn't actually look like an ant, but rather it is the same size as one, so that gives you an indication of just how small this entire thing has turned out to be.

That is One Hungry Komodo Dragon

The Komodo Dragon is pretty scary to look at, and it is certainly a deadly lizard. This thing is massive, and if you are caught up in its path, you had better be fast and able to get out of the way almost immediately.

However, it is not their size or the bacteria that exists in their mouth that would probably kill you, but rather how much they can eat in a short period of time. It turns out that these lizards are pretty hungry, and you can tell that by the way in which they are able to eat 5 pounds of meat in under a minute. Now, you just try and do that and see how difficult it is, and we have the meat prepared for us.

Basically, this lizard is a mean eating machine, so if you do come across one, you better hope it's not hungry.

The Rule of Thumb Concept

If you have ever heard of the 'rule of thumb' concept, then you may have already thought that it does come across as being a rather strange idea. After all, what does it mean and why is your thumb involved in this particular equation?

Well, it turns out that the answer to the origins of this phrase are a lot easier to understand than you may have initially expected. However, there is no doubt that the origins are not exactly PC for the world today.

To understand the phrase, we have to go back several centuries to an old English law. In the law, it stated that you could not beat your wife with anything wider than your thumb or else it would then be deemed to be cruel. Now, this is pretty shocking when you think about it, but then society was certainly different back in the not-so-good olden days.

Anyway, from that 'rule' about the width of your thumb, it then kind of stuck as a saying, with it then evolving into being used in a variety of ways. Perhaps now that you know the origins, you will think twice about how to go ahead and use it in your own life?

The English-Speaking Chinese

The English language is pretty much the global language now, but there are a number of facts surrounding it that may very well surprise people. Take China as a prime example because that one country has more English-speaking individuals than the whole of the United States.

That is quite mind-boggling, but then it makes more sense when you stop to really think about the population dynamics. You must remember that China has over one billion inhabitants, which is several times bigger than the United States. With that in mind, it becomes easier understand how this could all happen, but considering it is not their native language, it does make it a bit more spectacular.

Well, That Didn't Take Long

When you think of war, it is probably going to be the case that you will automatically think of something that just seems to drag on for what appears to be an eternity. However, it has not always been like that when you look at history.

Of course, if you go back centuries then there are 'wars' that lasted a few days, but we do prefer to refer to them as battles rather than anything else. To most, they are something that is completely different. But then, what do you think is the shortest war in history?

The answer is going to be different from what most people think, and to get the answer we need to go back to 1896 and head off to deepest and darkest Africa. The countries in question were Zanzibar and Great Britain, and even though this was just one of many wars that the UK would fight in Africa around this time, there is no doubt that this particular one was not what anybody would have expected.

You see, the war between these two nations lasted a grand total of 38 minutes before Zanzibar started to think better about what they were doing and decided to surrender. It is hard to believe that it was even worth their time and effort getting started with this war considering it was over so quickly. You are going to find it difficult to ever find another war at any point in human history that is ever going to stand a chance of beating this one in the time stakes.

Happy Birthday to All of You

Your birthday is always the best day of the year for you when your family and friends make you feel that bit more special than normal. For some, it makes them feel as if they are on top of the world and nobody else actually matters at any point.

However, what if there was a solitary fact that may very well remove some of the gloss from the day? What if you discovered that your special day was not quite as special as you perhaps thought?

Relax, it's not as bad as you think, simply because the fact in question is connected to the number of people that share your birthday with you. After all, you never thought that it was just you that was born on that day, did you?

Even though there are no exact figures, it is believed that at least nine million people, with the figure rising every year, share the same birthday as you. That is a lot of people, but then it is also going to account for a lot of candles and birthday cake as well.

Getting Fat on Stamps

Even though sending an old-fashioned letter seems to be a thing of the past, there are still some people out there that know what a stamp is and what it is used for. However, there is one fact about the stamp that the majority of people are going to be unaware of, and it is a fact that is actually pretty cool all on its own.

If you get any stamp and do the customary thing of licking the back of it, then in the process of doing so you are consuming 1/10th of a calorie. Okay, so it would involve you licking a number of stamps to build up those calories, and the taste would be horrible, but it is all to do with the sticky resin that is on the back of them. When you think about it, this also shows you how easy it is to build up the calories even when you are not aware that you are doing so.

Urine Trouble Now Pussycat

Urine—we all produce it, and it is a natural part of our body and the way in which it works. The same goes for every animal that is out there as well, but not all urine is the same.

To illustrate what we mean, we can turn to the rather humble cat because their urine is capable of doing something that is rather different and outlandish compared to what is produced by other animals. You see, if you have the correct kind of black light, then what you will find is that the urine produced by a cat is going to actually glow in the dark. Now, that is going to be a pretty cool party trick for anybody to do, but then the cat is hardly going to be able to boast about it to all of its friends, is it?

You are Always Quite Close to the Sea in England

For large countries, it is very possible for you to be a substantial distance away from the sea, but that is not the case in England. Of course, the fact that the United Kingdom is an island does make life a whole lot easier, but even then, you may be surprised to discover just how close you are always going to be from the sea, no matter where in the country you are located.

While parts of Canada or the United States can be an absolute eternity away from the sea, you are never more than 75 miles from the sea anywhere in the UK. Yes, you can pretty much drive there in next to no time and be dipping your toes in the ice-cold water, and all before it is time for lunch.

Now, that's not to say that the actual beach itself will be worthy of you spending time there because that is probably not true. However, if you are just looking for that bracing sea air, then it really is quite close to hand.

That Shrimp Packs a Punch

The humble shrimp is not exactly the kind of animal that you feel you should be afraid of, but what would you think if we told you that a certain kind of shrimp is able to really pack a punch?

Now, this is clearly all relative to its size, but the outcome is still going to be pretty impressive even just for us humans, as we could never imagine reaching such stunning and amazing heights. But then, what are we talking about?

Well, the Peacock Mantis Shrimp has the insane ability to throw a punch at a speed of 50 mph. In addition, the punch accelerates faster than a .22 bullet, so you literally would feel it before you were able to see it. Obviously, there is no real need for us to worry too much about being punched by a shrimp, as that would be the strangest thing to have ever happened, but it does give you some insight into what the animal kingdom is capable of doing.

That Pigeon Loves its Art

The pigeon is seen by many as being nothing more than an absolute pest and flying vermin. However, they are certainly far more intelligent than we are perhaps willing to give them credit for.

We all know that certain pigeons have the ability to find their way back home and to even beat others in a race, but it seems that their intelligence goes far beyond even that. Instead, trained pigeons have a strange sense of art, as has been shown in a variety of studies. What it has shown is that a pigeon that has been trained can actually identify the differences between paintings by Monet and Picasso. Why it has been decided that those two artists would be the favorite for pigeons is unknown, as is the ones that they seem to prefer, but they are certainly more than capable of distinguishing between the two.

Now, if you ever see a pigeon the next time that you are in an art gallery, just think that they may very well be in there doing some research and indulging in their love for art.

Chicken Tikka Masala is Not Indian

Chicken tikka masala is a spicy curry dish, but it's not Indian. Nor is it from any of those other countries that are often regarded as being the proverbial hotbed of curry dishes.

Instead, it comes from the UK, and it is absolutely not an Indian dish, at least in its origins. The people in the UK love it, and even though there are various claims as to the places that actually created it, the one thing that is certain is that this curry dish was recently named as the national dish of the UK.

You have to admit that this is strange as there are a whole host of other dishes that you would have put before this as an option.

As Drunk as a Chimp

There is this rather strange concept that it is only we humans that are capable of getting drunk, but science has shown that this is completely wrong. Instead, we can look to one of our rather close relatives, the humble chimp, to see that they too appear to have a particular taste for alcohol.

Of course, they are not going out there and brewing some kind of alcohol in the way that we do, but they are still able to get pretty drunk just by using things that are around them. In particular, we are talking about chimps in Guinea that have a particular favorite when it comes to what they want to drink. They seem to have a preference for fermented palm sap, and even though it may not sound as if it is too pleasant, it does contain around 3% alcohol, so it is on a par with some light beers that are out there on the market.

This isn't to say that the chimps are having a party and getting drunk on a regular basis, as that's not the case, but it does give you a completely different sense of what chimps could get up to in their free time.

Firefox isn't a Fox

Firefox is clearly one of the most popular web browsers around, but there is one fact about it that is going to confuse people because it seems that we have all been wrong in one small area.

You would automatically think that as it was called Firefox that the animal in the logo is a fox, but that is not actually true. Yes, that thing that looks like a fox and seems to be called a fox is not actually a fox.

So, what is it??

Well, the answer is more straightforward than you think because it is actually a red panda. Okay, so that has probably just confused you even more, so a further explanation is going to be required.

The red panda is an animal that is native to parts of the Himalayas, as well as just over the border in China. In English, the name translates from the Chinese into the word 'firefox' and it is from that translation that we get the name of the browser. So, the next time someone mentions the browser, you can then astound them with the story of how it should be called Red Panda.

Google and Their Goats

When you have a large HQ that is surrounded by gorgeous green grass, then looking after it may become rather tiring. However, when you are a company that is as large as Google, you might believe that, as money is no option, they would just hire somebody to come and cut it for them on a regular basis.

Well, that is what they do, but they do not rely purely on human beings to help them out with this, because Google being Google, they want to do things slightly different than the norm. This has ultimately led to them renting a number of goats. Yes, they do actually rent goats from a company called California Grazing.

Now, the job at hand for these goats is less about the grass—though they will certainly munch away on it when they can—and more about the various weeds and brush that surrounds their HQ. By allowing the goats to feast on it, kind of like an all-you-can-eat deal for them, it helps to keep their surroundings neat and tidy without it having a negative impact on their carbon footprint.

A Terrifying Crocodile

When it comes to animals, there are perhaps few out there that can create such a sense of fear and terror as the crocodile. These living dinosaurs are not the kind of animal that you want to mess around with simply because if they want to eat you, there is little that you can do to stop them.

However, they are certainly better in the water than out of it, so in those instances you would stand a chance of getting away, but that has not always been the case.

Instead, if we go back to the time of the dinosaurs and the area that we now know as North Africa, there was a type of crocodile that was just designed to terrify other dinosaurs. To be honest, we should be eternally grateful that it became extinct, as the thought of sharing the world with this species is just not worth thinking about.

The reason for that is due to fossil hunters having discovered the remains of a crocodile that could actually gallop. Yes, it was just as good out of the water as it was when it was in it, so how lucky were we that we avoided it?

It seems that this species, known as Kaprosuchus saharicus, was quite a good runner as well, so the other dinosaurs in the area had very little chance of escaping them. You have to admit that catching this kind of animal would make for a very different program on Nat Geo Wild.

Is Bill Gates a Traitor?

Bill Gates needs no introduction, as he has only been one of the founders of Microsoft and the richest man in the world for longer than we care to remember. However, what would you say if we could tell you that the one and only Bill Gates could very well be a traitor?

Well, it's not strictly true because it seems that even though he created Windows, when it came to his bespoke home being built, the architects either had no idea that they were going to see the real Bill Gates or they had no access to a Windows computer. Ultimately, it means that the house for Bill Gates was originally designed using an Apple computer.

Yes, for the designing aspect, the job was given over to the competition, and this should have led to a number of important developments as it allowed Gates to see where his technology was falling short. He does now have one of the most hi-tech homes in the world, but it must be slightly annoying that it was designed on a computer from the one company that is his main rival.

The Queen of Swans

You would think that the Queen of England has more than enough things to own, from priceless works of art to countless palaces, as well as vast sums of money. However, it seems that even this is not enough because of a relatively unknown law that appears to want to give her even more than the Queen herself had bargained for.

The law is focused on just one type of animal, well a bird, to be precise. You see, according to UK law, the Queen owns every single unmarked mute swan that is in open water throughout the country. Quite what she is expected to do with all of those swans is open to interpretation, as is the very reason as to why this law should exist in the first place.

It's hardly going to be the case that she is able to look after them, as we are talking about wild birds, but it does then mean that as they are the property of the crown, they do have a certain amount of legal protection. So, if you are a swan, then that is probably a good thing—even though us humans are unable to make sense of it.

Not All Bats are Blind

You have probably heard of the phrase 'as blind as a bat' and even though it is true for most species of bat, it is not something that is universal. Instead, people are surprised to discover that one of the more common species of bat is actually not blind at all.

For this, we are talking about the fruit bat, and while other bats use echolocation in order to find their way around, that does not apply in this instance. Instead, what we have is a bat that actually uses its sense of sight as well as smell to make sure that they can navigate without any problems.

The very idea of a bat that can see goes against pretty much everything that we have ever believed about this kind of animal, but at least the next time somebody tells you that you are as blind as a bat, you can tell them you are a fruit bat instead.

This Fight Stinks!

It's not exactly going to be any surprise to discover that the animal kingdom does have a variety of ways of allowing animals to have a fight. They are hardly going to do things in the normal manner compared to us humans, but then when you find out what happens in some instances, that is going to be a good thing.

Take the ring-tailed lemur as an example. When two males get together in order to sort out their differences, they do something rather peculiar, and we should be quite happy that we humans don't follow their lead. You see, they have what is commonly known as a 'stink fight', and it is exactly as it sounds.

The two males will spend their time throwing scent at one another, and it's not exactly known for being that pleasant either. They basically try to out smell each other until one decides that its sense of smell can take it no longer, leaving the other as the victor. You must admit that boxing would be different if that was how the bout was decided.

That Sentence is for the Dogs

You must admit that the judicial system has had a few ups and downs with some rather strange sentences being handed down for strange crimes. However, you would be hard-pressed to find a sentence that could actually beat this one for being completely bizarre.

To get to grips with the sentence, we have to go back in time to 1924 and to the Eastern State Penitentiary. Now, the location itself is not going to throw up any strange situations, because you would expect a prison to be filled with individuals with varying sentences, but this is different.

The difference on this occasion was that the prisoner was actually a dog. Not just any dog, but one that was, in the eyes of the governor, guilty of the most horrific crime ever committed—a crime that could only then lead to the harshest punishment that they could hand out at that moment in time, life in prison without the possibility of parole.

Yes, this dog was sent to prison for the rest of its life because it had managed to kill the cat that belonged to the governor. So incensed, the governor then decided that it was best that the dog never saw the light of day again, and it was locked up. We told you that it was the strangest sentence that we could find.

A Cat Doesn't Have a Sweet Tooth

Cats are known for being rather particular when it comes to knowing what they like to eat, but it seems that it is not all going to be decided by themselves. Instead, nature works against them from time to time, and that then ultimately leads to them having to make certain decisions as to what tastes they prefer.

Now, we all know that they go absolutely insane for certain things such as catnip, but give your cat some sugar and it is going to look at you in a strange way. Why? Well, it turns out that cats do not have sweet taste buds, so they have no idea what sugar or anything sweet actually tastes like, as they just cannot appreciate it in the same way.

So, if you own a cat, stick to the salty and meaty things, as they are going to love you more for it rather than being given something that has no taste whatsoever.

The Surfing Duck

Ducks are pretty cool in their own way, but it seems that they have been spotted doing something that takes their coolness levels to completely new heights.

So, what is this thing that we talk about that we believe will leave you feeling completely amazed? Well, it is the idea of a surfing duck. Yes, a surfing duck, and if that has not left you sitting there stunned, then who knows what would make you speechless.

In various studies, ducks have been observed basically riding waves like a surfer and then going back out in order to do it again on the water. Quite what they are getting out of this is still unknown, but it has been observed often enough to know that it is not just a fluke or a strange phenomenon, but that it is something that they genuinely seem to enjoy doing.

That STD Has a Buzz about it

The idea of us humans picking up an STD is never nice to contemplate, but if you believed that it was only us that were able to get them, then think again. However, if we did ask you which animal you would think was also able to pick up an STD, most people would probably go along the lines of another ape due to us being very close in nature, and that would be the sensible option.

But then, you would be wrong.

Instead, it is the honeybee that can also go ahead and pick up an STD, and you would have probably sat there for days before you eventually picked the humble bee. Of course, it should not put you off your honey, but it makes you wonder what else those bees are getting up to if they are able to spread this kind of disease throughout their colony.

The British and Their Tea

Everybody knows that the British love their tea, but then it is also interesting to find out the extent to which they seem to allow this hot drink to just take over their lives. It is estimated that on any given day in the UK that the Brits consume in the region of 165 million cups of tea, which is a crazy amount when you think about it.

To show how they love it so much, that figure is more than 20 times the daily amount that is consumed in the United States, which has several times the population. Of course, the US is known as being more of a coffee country, but even with that taken into consideration, it is still a huge amount of tea for one country to drink in a single day.

South Korea and the Turd

South Korea is a country that is known for its technology and ability to invent new things, but there is something about the culture that is just strange, and it could very well change your opinion of them in general.

It seems that South Koreans have an absolute fascination with turds, and there is just no other way of stating it. This obsession with a certain thing that we do with our body has moved into a different part of their culture. It includes phone charms in the shape of turds and also cookies that are shaped like them (but don't taste like it.) They have a museum dedicated to this bodily function in the country, and have even installed toilets that play pleasant music.

Now, perhaps there are certain things that can be taken from it, such as the nice background music, but turd-shaped cookies has to be taking things to a completely new level.

Men and Makeup

The idea of men wearing makeup is something that has had a bit of a boom in recent years, and none more so than in South Korea. It seems that guys in the country absolutely love wearing it to such an extent that they spend in the region of $1 billion every single year, which makes them the biggest spenders in the world in this particular market.

Not only that, but they say that as much as 20% of all South Korean men state that they use makeup on a regular basis, which is also a huge percentage when compared to anywhere else. It is not quite certain as to why they seem to have this kind of fascination with it, but there is no doubt that it is an industry that is growing, so if you want to show off about your beauty knowledge, this is one fact that is probably going to end up stopping the conversation in its tracks.

The Plastic Surgery Capital of the World

Staying with the beauty idea for a moment, which country do you think is going to be the effective capital of the world when it comes to plastic surgery? At first, there will probably be a number of potential contenders, but we are talking about when it comes to the per capita concept in order to determine who the winner is.

You would think that parts of the US or Europe would be the main hub of plastic surgery, but if you did indeed think that, then you would be wrong. Instead, the capital of the world when it comes to plastic surgery is actually South Korea, and they are way out in front compared to other countries in the world.

It is believed that as many as one in every three women in Seoul alone have had some kind of plastic surgery procedure carried out, and a lot of them have had more than just that single operation. It means that the cosmetic surgery market in South Korea is not just booming, but it is increasing in popularity to such an extent that it is certainly becoming very common for individuals to just go out and have something done just to feel as if they are part of the crowd.

Your Brain is Faster than You Think

People will often get to a point in a the day where they feel as if their brain is working slower than it normally is, but then at what speed do you think that your brain actually does work? The answer is going to be rather surprising, and it does help to show just how amazing your brain is.

Of course, what we are talking about here are the messages that are sent along the nerves, as it is their ability to move along these networks that basically allows us to function. You might be surprised to hear that those messages travel at a speed of 200 mph, which you have to admit is mightily impressive. Also, that speed never changes, so the next time that you think your brain is working slowly, it is just not possible, as it is pretty consistent when it comes to the speed side of things.

That is a Lot of DNA

The human body is amazing in the things that it seems to be able to contain within it that just do not make any sense whatsoever. Take your DNA as an example.

Your DNA is in a coil, but what would happen if you uncoiled it and then stretched out all of the DNA that is your body? How far do you think it would be able to reach?

The DNA is actually around 8.5 cm long, and yet it is able to be packed into a space so small that you cannot see it without some kind of assistance. If you then unpacked all of your DNA, it means that it would stretch for an absolutely staggering 744 million miles. To put that into some kind of perspective, that means that it is roughly the same as from the earth to the planet Saturn, and that is hardly the kind of place that you could just walk to.

Now, think about how it is even possible for all of that to be contained inside your body, and it starts to give you a better impression of just how amazing your body is and the way in which we seem to be able to pack so much into a small space.

So, the next time somebody tells you how far your intestines would stretch, or any other strange fact about the body, perhaps you should then usurp them by giving them this one stunning fact all about your DNA.

You Really Have a Filthy Mouth

If anybody has ever told you that you have a filthy mouth, then technically they are telling the truth even though they are not aware of this fact. Of course, they are referring to something you have said, usually foul language, but that is not the reason as to why you do indeed have a filthy mouth.

Instead, the fact that we have a filthy mouth, which correlates to you having such a dirty and unhygienic mouth, is due to the number of bacteria present in our mouth. We are talking about billions of bacteria in our mouth, but that does not have to mean that every single bacterium is bad, as that is certainly not the case. Actually, we all have more bacteria in our mouth than the number of people alive in the world today, and when you consider that this is billions of people, it does make you think about how packed our mouths are.

Now, you don't have to stress or worry about this, or go and wash your mouth out, because it's not going to do you any harm, but the next time somebody tells you that you have a filthy mouth, hit them with this fact, as it will stop them in their tracks.

Tasting Faster than We Can See

We are always amazed by what our body is able to achieve and the speed at which it can do various things, but this next fact is going to make you wonder what else it may be capable of achieving. You might think that one of the fastest things that our body can do is for our eyes to blink, and even though it is indeed fast, there are a number of things that can beat it. One such feat is actually our ability to taste things because it has been shown that our body can identify taste in only 0.0015 seconds, which you have to admit is seriously impressive.

So, the next time you see somebody tasting something for the first time only to immediately recoil in horror, don't think that they are just putting on an act, as that is not the case. Instead, they are merely reacting in the same length of time it takes for their body to identify the taste in the first place, so perhaps they actually are telling the truth.

The Whales with an Accent

As humans, we are very used to the concept of having a regional accent, and we can end up being pretty good at identifying them, at least those that are more common. However, we are not the only members of the animal kingdom that have this ability to speak with a regional accent.

Instead, certain species of whales also have this ability, and in particular the Caribbean sperm whale. It has been shown in studies that they do indeed have regional accents, and this has been identified by scientists as being completely different to sperm whales from other parts of the world.

It does then open up the possibility that even more animals actually have these regional accents than we are used to identifying, but at least we are not alone in this respect.

The Cube Poop

After the earlier fact about South Korea and their fascination with poop, this fact should be absolutely perfect for them, even though anybody should find this rather interesting.

For this poop fact, we are going to look at the wombat because they are able to achieve something that is pretty remarkable— if anything related to this bodily function can be deemed to be remarkable. You see, they do not produce poop like any other animal. Instead, they have this strange ability to produce poop that is basically cube shaped. Quite why is unknown, but it does make you wonder if the wombat has a cube shaped butt that would then allow it to produce such a strange shape.

How to Keep Flies Away From You

Flies are annoying, and it can often feel as if they are just never to leave you alone, which is then going to drive you insane. However, an ancient Egyptian Pharaoh came up with his very own idea that apparently worked even though we would not go ahead and recommend it as an option.

Pharaoh Pepi II came up with the idea that flies loved honey, so if you had something covered in honey, it would attract the flies and they would then leave you alone. You must admit that it sounds perfectly plausible as an option, but he did then go ahead and do something a bit different to what we would recommend.

Instead, of getting various objects and smearing them in honey, the Pharaoh would have some slaves stripped naked and then covered in honey to use as bait for the flies. They would then have to literally hang around the King whenever he wanted them to so the flies would leave him alone and he could live in peace. Of course, this would now go against so many laws in any country you care to mention, but then if you were also the King of somewhere, the laws may not really apply.

The King with the Most Children

If we can stay in Ancient Egypt for just a few minutes, we can look at their history and see that a Pharaoh could also lay claim to being the King with the most children during his reign. We are not just talking about a handful of children either, as it goes far beyond that.

The King in question was Ramses II, who was seen by many as being the greatest King to have ever existed. He ruled for more than 60 years, but it does appear to be the case that he had more than enough things to do in order to keep him occupied.

It is said that he fathered more than 90 children during his reign, which is quite impressive when you think about it, and the results were split pretty evenly between boys and girls, even though exact numbers are still unknown.

It does make other rulers pale into apparent insignificance when it comes to their extended family.

Where Do Your Organs Come From?

We are all familiar with the concept of our vital organs, but have you ever wondered why they are called organs in the first place? Well, the answer takes us to Greece, which should be no surprise considering so many medical terms are either Greek or Roman in origin.

In this instance, the term 'organ' comes from the Greek word 'organon', which roughly translates as meaning either tool or instrument. You would think that there should have been a better option available when it came to choosing a word to represent our heart, lungs, and so on, but then they are all instruments that keep us going, so perhaps it is more accurate than we would like to think.

Where Do Your Muscles Come From?

For a moment, let us stick to the idea of the origins of words for this fact, only change locations and move from ancient Greece to ancient Rome. Once again, it is a medical term, and one that we all use without giving much thought as to where it comes from.

The word in this instance is 'muscle', and we all know that we have a huge number of muscles in our body and that they help us to move around, but what is the origin of the word? Actually, it comes from the Latin term 'musculus', and this translates as 'little mouse' which is very strange and appears to have no relation to the muscles in our body.

However, the use of the word originates from what the Romans thought that the way in which you can see certain muscles moving in the body was similar to the way a mouse would move. In other words, they started to link it with the idea of all of these small mice under your skin helping your body to work, which is clearly wrong, but it is still a cool story that explains where the term comes from.

The Male Tank and the Female Tank

The very idea of a tank being assigned a sex is, well, rather strange to say the least. However, that is exactly what happened during World War I. It turns out that the British army decided to identify tanks by sex, but it was merely done to distinguish between two types of tanks that had different strengths to one another. In other words, it was not as insane as you may have initially thought.

It turns out that the male tank had cannons installed as their main weapon, whereas the female tank used a heavy machine gun as the primary weapon. Each one could then be employed in various situations, but the gender-specific tank was not something that would last for too long a period of time, as it was then decided that a tank should just be a tank and nothing else.

The Role of the Messenger Dog

The battles of World War I were horrific, and being on the frontline in the trenches was not the kind of place that you would want to be. Communications were still very basic, but what do you think was used in order to get messages to the front?

You would have initially thought that carrier pigeons would have been the main choice, but that was not the case, as it was deemed that there was too much risk involved in them being shot down or simply not being trained well enough. Instead, the dog was used in most instances as they were regarded as being far more reliable. A message would be added to a canister that would then be tied around the neck of the dog before it was set off on its merry way to the frontline through the network of trenches. Once it arrived, the canister was opened, and any reply was then inserted back into the canister before the dog was sent back to safety.

But that was not all that they were used for in the war, as they were seen as being extremely important in a number of ways. For example, the dog was also used to lay down a number of telegraph wires. They were viewed as being easier to replace than a soldier who would be in absolute danger as soon as they stuck their head above the trench for even a second. It is unknown how many dogs effectively gave up their lives for the battle.

Which War Claimed the Most American Lives?

The United States has been in a number of wars throughout its history, but which one actually claimed the most lives? You do have a range of contenders to choose from, and most people would select World War I or II, or perhaps even Vietnam as the one with the most deaths.

However, if you did choose any of those options, then you would be very, very wrong.

Instead, the war that claimed the most American lives was the American Civil War. In fact, it claimed far more lives than the other wars all added together, which is certainly something that is going to surprise a number of people.

Overall, it is believed that as many as 618,000 people died during the Civil War, and this accounted for approximately 2% of the entire population at the time, which really is a huge number. The other wars just do not even come close to that number of deaths. However, it should be added that a number of the deaths were caused by disease, and it was not helped along by the way in which society had been negatively affected by the war, so even though they may not have been caused by being in battle, the deaths can still be attributed to the fighting.

Who Lost the Most Men in WW2?

There are all kinds of different statistics regarding war, and it's fair to say that some of them are far more shocking than others. Take this one as a perfect example.

Out of all of the different countries that took part in World War II, which one lost the most men, and how many did they lose? Now, a lot of people are going to correctly guess the Soviet Union, as it was the country with the largest population, so it makes sense that they could lose the most men, but the scale of it all is astonishing.

It is believed that out of all of the men born in the Soviet Union in 1923, that 80% of them did not get to see the end of the war as a result of them being killed in action. In total, it is believed that as many as 21 million people from the Soviet Union lost their lives in this war, making them far and away the country with the most casualties. But then, it was certainly not all one-way traffic for them because it is also known that out of every five German soldiers that were killed in the war, four actually died on the Eastern Front. That is why it was the one place that you did not want to be sent to if you were in the German army.

How Did Egypt Get its Name?

Ancient Egypt is something that is known around the world, but the Egyptians themselves did not generally refer to themselves by that moniker. Instead, the civilization was known by different names throughout its history, and it is not until we get to the Greeks that some name that signifies Egypt was actually created.

Back in its earliest times, known as the Old Kingdom, it was known by the name 'Kemer', which also means 'Black Land'. This was due to the color of the soil around the Nile, which became the source of life for the entire civilization.

However, it then changed its name to 'Deshret' which stands for 'Red Land', and that is in direct reference to the red sand that makes up the majority of the land. It would then be known later on in its history by the name 'Hwt-ka-Ptah' which means 'House of the Ka and Ptah' with Ptah being known as one of the earliest Gods to appear in their history. Eventually, the Greeks then came along and took control, with it then being given the name Aegyptus, and you can now see where we get the English name.

The Problem with the Shortest Day of the Year

Even though you may not know too much about the shortest day of the year, it stands to reason that it would make sense for you to feel that this would be the point where the earth is the furthest point away from the sun. After all, it would mean that it was darker for longer if this was the case, but the problem with that approach is simply that the sun and the earth are not willing to play ball.

In actual fact, the day of the winter solstice is actually the point where the earth and the sun are at their closest, and this just simply goes against absolutely everything and anything that seems to make sense in the world. This is all connected to angles and the rotation of the earth, so if you want to blame anything for this bizarre point, then blame physics.

The Most Expensive Olympic Games Ever

The cost associated with hosting the Olympic Games has been known to be growing at a crazy rate over the last few decades.

It is often the case that the countries, or even just the cities alone, end up in debt as a direct result of being given this apparent accolade of being the host city.

However, what would you guess as being the most expensive summer Olympic Games ever hosted? There is a pretty good chance that most people would argue that it was connected to the last one held because surely the costs are just going to continue to rise every single time?

Well, that is not the case. Instead, the most expensive games held were in 2008 in Beijing, where it cost an absolutely mind-blowing $40 billion. However, that is not the most expensive games ever if you include the winter versions, as that accolade goes to Russia for the 2014 games in Sochi. The crazy thing is that the Russian games cost more than $40 billion, yet the games in Beijing held more than three times the number of events, which just shows how Russia vastly overpaid for the honor.

Who Invented Champagne?

If somebody was to ask you who invented Champagne, then you may not know the name of the individual in question, but you would more than likely say that it was some individual in France. But then, if that was your answer, it is sadly going to be wrong.

Yes, a drink that is famously French is not even French in origin, and what makes it worse for France is that it is believed that the process itself was invented in England, their major enemy for so many things over the centuries.

The person in question was known by the name of Christopher Merret, who was a scientist in 1662. He was never actually intending to put bubbles into wine, as that was more of a by-product in general, but it seems that after stumbling across this creation that he found it was pretty good. Of course, the French then caught wind of the techniques that were being used by Merret and imported them across the English Channel and into the Champagne region. Ultimately, it was then given the French name, and Merret was largely forgotten.

That is One Big Wedding

People around the world seem to have a fascination for the British royal family, so when Prince William was getting married to Kate Middleton, it was quite a big deal. However, you might be stunned as to how big a deal it was around the world, and to get a better understanding of it all, we need to check out the viewing figures according to different television stations.

When we do this, what we see is that more than two billion people around the world watched the wedding on their television, which is crazy, as it means that roughly one in every four people alive in the world took the time to watch it even when they lived in various time zones. It literally did make the world stop in its tracks, making it one of the most watched events of this kind to have ever happened.

So, when somebody asks you about the number of witnesses at a wedding, perhaps tell them that the answer is two billion just to confuse them.

What is the Largest Snowman Ever Built?

Kids, and this includes grown-up kids, just seem to love the idea of building a snowman, but we are often limited as to the size that we can produce simply because of the amount of snow available and also how tall we are. But then, what would happen if there were fewer limitations and you had the opportunity to build a huge snowman? How big would you need to go in order to beat the record for the largest one ever?

Well, you are going to require a serious amount of snow, and that is because the largest snowman ever created was in Bethel, Maine, and it was built in February 1999. The size? 113 feet and 7 inches. Just think about that for a second, as that is one seriously big snowman, but then it also makes you wonder as to how big the carrot would have to be for his nose or how long the scarf would have to be to then wrap around him.

Now when it snows for you, go and see how close to the record you can get, but then you are going to require a lot of snow and a whole lot of help.

Who was the First American Serial Killer?

There tends to be something inherently fascinating about serial killers, but do you know who the first American serial killer was reported to have been? Well, the answer, according to researchers, appears to have been a certain Dr. H.H. Holmes, who apparently confessed to committing a total of 27 murders back in the 1890s.

For Holmes, there seems to have been no sense of remorse for his killings, because to him it was just something that he was able to do, and he never gave it much thought. In fact, he once said that killing was just something that he did, just as a poet could not help themselves when it came to writing poetry.

Of course, he was not the worst serial killer to have ever emerged from the United States, but you have to admit that starting off with a guy that killed 27 people is pretty impressive.

The Sociopathic Family

Have you ever heard people talking about the way they grew up to be like one of their parents? This is often due to how certain things are inherited, but it does not always then equate to being something that you would want to go ahead and inherit.

In fact, if we look at the role of sociopaths, we see that things really can be in the genes and that your childhood environment can play a role in how you then grow up into an adult.

What has been noticed in various studies is that if a child is diagnosed as being sociopathic, then there is a very high risk that one of their parents is also sociopathic as well. Actually, the chances are 4 or 5 times higher than the average human being, which does show the way that your family acts can indeed make a difference to your future.

But one important point is that there has also been a study whereby they focused on people that were sociopathic and were also adopted as infants. Even then, there was a much higher rate whereby one of their biological relatives also had the personality disorder, even though they had been removed from that particular environment.

How Many Cars Exist on Earth?

The car is the most popular form of transport, and it is easy to understand why that is indeed the case. However, are you aware of just how many cars there are on earth being driven around at this moment in time?

Well, even though we do not know an exact number, it is fair to say that there are at least one billion cars right at this very moment. In other words, roughly one in eight people have a car, and when you consider the population that cannot afford one due to being in poverty, then that figure becomes even more surprising than before.

Of course, the spread of cars is also very uneven throughout the world, and the west certainly has more than one car for every eight people, but perhaps the scariest part of all is the way in which this figure is expected to continue growing, so there may be a time where we simply become swamped by cars in the world.

Use Your Head when Opening Your Car

This is one of those strange facts that you are probably going to go and try out simply because it sounds too good to be true. However, in order to do so, you need a car that has a remote-control locking device.

So, what do you need to do? Well, you need to open your car, but you will know that your remote control does have a limit when it comes to the distance from which it is able to operate. But, what do you think you could do in order to increase the range?

The answer is certainly far more bizarre than you would originally imagine because the answer has–to do with your head. Yes, if you go ahead and hold the remote control to your head, then you are going to be able to effectively double the distance that the remote control is able to work. The reason for this is simply because your skull works as an amplifier for the signal making it stronger over a longer distance.

You will probably want to go and check this out before you read the next fact or else it will drive you insane.

Keep Her Feet Warm

It will certainly come as no surprise to hear that cold weather is going to reduce your sexual desire by a significant amount, as it is almost as if our body and those sensations effectively shut down over the winter. However, there is one thing that you can do to help the woman in your relationship to reach orgasm, and it is going to sound very strange and even difficult for you to understand how to tell her about it in advance.

This key point focuses on her feet, but not in the way that you are probably thinking.

Instead, it has been shown in various studies that if you are able to make sure that her feet are warm, by whatever means necessary, then the woman is 30% more likely to orgasm. It is just a strange anomaly whereby the comfort and warmth associated with your feet being like toast allows the body and mind to relax into what is actually going on. So, if you want to show that you are indeed a great lover and that you have her best interests at heart, then make sure she has some warm socks on, as it is certainly going to help.

Why is Snow White in Color?

Everybody knows that snow is white in color, but do you actually know why it is white and not something else? Well, the answer to this question lies in the structure of the snowflake and the way in which snow is created. In other words, science and Mother Nature has the answer for you.

It turns out that the white color is all because of the crystals that make up the snowflake. Each crystal is actually translucent in nature, but it is the way in which it bounces light around that then leads to us seeing it as white. The light reacts with the crystals and produces light in different frequencies. This combination results in the white color that we all know and love so much, so nature is to thank for the color of snow.

What is the New Car Smell?

There seems to be something so enjoyable about the new car smell because so many of us love it, and we do so for a whole host of reasons. However, it may not all be just as good as we perhaps had hoped.

The problem is that the new car smell that you are loving is actually toxic, so that may very well change your opinion of how you perceive it. The reason for this is that it is the direct combination of over 50 different organic compounds and chemicals that are used in the production of the car, and it does take some time for it to go ahead and settle down to the point where we no longer smell it. However, this combination is not actually healthy for us.

It might not cause us too many issues, but there is a very real potential of it making us feel ill, which is not exactly something that you want to have happen to you when you have a new car to explore and have fun with.

Just remember that when the car salesman is pushing you for that sale and tells you the new car line so that you can throw it back at them for pushing something toxic to you.

What were the Youngest and Oldest Soldiers in the American Civil War?

To say that the soldiers that appeared in the American Civil War varied in age is a real understatement. However, do you know what that age range actually was?

The chances are that you will be taken aback by the difference, as it far outstrips any other war that happened before or since. The reason why we can say that with such confidence? Simply because it is known that the youngest soldier was a nine-years-old while the oldest was 80.

The boy came from Mississippi, while the oldest soldier came from Iowa, but they were not alone in their ages. Actually, the Civil War was also known as the 'boys war' simply because more than 10,000 soldiers on the Union side were under the age of 18 when they were sent into battle. Once again, that is higher than anything else that has since happened when it comes to war, and you just know that a large percentage of them were killed as a result.

How the SS Took Items from Jews and Hid Them

The Nazis are infamous for having taken wealth in various forms from European Jews that were living in areas under their control, but at the same time, most people are also aware that this wealth ended up in different accounts or vaults in a variety of locations.

But, how did they manage to do this without it looking too suspicious, allowing them to keep so much of it hidden after the war itself had ended?

The way in which the SS faction tackled this issue was by having everything under the name Max Helliger, and his name was ultimately used to open bank accounts that were then used to make deposits of gold, jewels, and anything else that they believed would be of worth to them later on. However, if you are wondering about who this Max Helliger is, and perhaps assuming that he was some individual within the Nazis, then you would be wrong.

Instead, the name was completely fictitious, and it was only created for the sole purpose of being able to create these bank accounts that would then allow them to make deposits. While there probably is a guy by that name alive today, the SS did not appear to go ahead and steal the identity of an individual just for this purpose. It seems that they just went down the fake road from the outset.

The Monarch Butterfly Knows What It Likes

People are used to birds migrating for the winter as they move to warmer climates in order to survive, but the Monarch butterfly is able to do things just as well as the average bird.

For butterflies in the United States, they are known to migrate to Mexico for the winter, with the average distance covered being in the region of 2,500 miles. Not only that, but it has been shown that when they get to their destination, the Monarch butterfly also enjoys hibernating, but they can only really do so when they are in the same tree as they were the year before.

In other words, if you are ever told that only birds migrate, then you can let people know about this species of butterfly, as it is the only insect that does this. Others just try and get through winter or end up dying as a result of their reluctance to migrate, even if it is just for a few months of the year.

Why is it 007?

When it comes to a superspy, then can there be a more famous one than James Bond? However, have you ever stopped to think about the reasons why he is known as 007?

Well, it turns out that the reason for that number being used as some kind of code is far more mundane than Bond himself would care to admit to, and it is all thanks to the creator, Ian Fleming. Now, you might think that he sat long and hard about codenames or spent time doing his research into how the Secret Service actually operated before settling on that code, but that would not be correct.

Instead, it seems that the 007 just represented the number of the bus that Fleming used to catch when he would travel from Canterbury into London. You can see how this knowledge does somewhat dilute the power of the number because James Bond is not then as cool as we perhaps initially imagined when you know that he was effectively named after an everyday bus route.

Anybody for Strawberries and Cream?

If you love tennis, then Wimbledon is going to be one of the highlights of your year, but aside from the sport and the inevitable rain, it is also famous for something else—strawberries and cream. It seems that those individuals that are lucky enough to get tickets to watch tennis at the tournament also love the tradition of strawberries and cream, but you would be amazed at how much they are able to consume over the course of two weeks.

Even though it does vary from year to year, the average amount of strawberries consumed every single year comes to approximately 27 tons, and for the cream there is a total of 7,000 liters. You have to admit that this is an impressive amount for people to eat, and they are charged a small fortune for the honor of doing so as well.

So, if you feel like trying some strawberries and cream, Wimbledon is the place to go, but just remember that it is only open for two weeks in the year, so it's best that you act fast.

Who Used to Have Harrods Close Their Doors?

When it comes to a shopping experience in the UK that is famous around the world, then heading off to Harrods in London is the place to go. However, the only problem that you will tend to face is the way in which it appears to be packed with people simply wishing to have the experience of being there even if they have no intention of buying anything.

To be honest, it is so busy that you would struggle to really absorb what is available, but that never used to be a problem for one person in particular.

So, who is that person? Well, it can only be the Queen herself because it used to be the case that Harrods would close its doors for one day to allow the Queen to go ahead and do her Christmas shopping in peace. Of course, there were also security issues to contend with, which ultimately led to them closing their doors, but it would certainly make life a whole lot easier if we were all given that honor whenever we wished to do some shopping.

Who is the Real Robin Hood?

Robin Hood is seen by many as being the perfect example of someone standing up for those less fortunate than they are, but who exactly was the real Robin Hood?

Sadly, the truth is going to be rather disappointing for so many people because there was not actually a real individual by that name. Instead, what we have is a story that is a combination of pieces of information about different outlaws that existed in and around England at the same time. Their stories would then be entwined together by minstrels who were present at the court of an influential landowner where they would regale guests with the daring tale of this individual, when they were really talking about various people.

In fact, the Robin Hood theory only appeared at the end of the 16th century, and it was thanks to a playwright by the name of Antony Munday. It seems that he was the one who was responsible for turning him into a Saxon Earl, and it may have even been done due to political reasons at the time. Apparently, the landed gentry were rather upset with the way in which power was being diluted, so Munday created the character as a direct response, as well as to act as a warning to others that bad things can happen to even the richest in society if they are not careful.

So, in other words, it was not actually Kevin Costner.

Imagine Writing this as Your Address

When it comes to entering your address, we can often wish that we lived in a place with a short name simply because we are very lazy and do not want to spend any time typing or writing in this information. So, imagine if you lived in a place in Thailand that has the longest city name in the world. How long is the name? Well, according to some individuals, as there appears to be different spellings, it is a staggering 163 letters long.

Of course, the name is actually made up of different words that ultimately provide a description of the place, but the Thai authorities took things to a whole new level when they came up with this name. So, deep breath because here we go.

The name of the town is: Krungthepmahanakornamornratana kosinmahintarayutthayamahadilokphopnopparatrajathanibur iromudomrajaniwesmahasatharnamornphimarnavatarnsathit sakkattiyavisanukamprasit.

You must admit that this is a bit of a mouthful, but it then translates into something along the lines of 'The great city of angels, the supreme unconquerable land of the great immortal divinity, the royal capital of nine noble gems, the pleasant city, with plenty of grand royal palaces and divine paradises for the reincarnated deity given by Indra and created by the god of crafting.'

Even with that translation it still sounds like a huge place name, so it is no surprise that people in Thailand do tend to shorten it to something that is far more manageable.

Where Does Halloween Come From?

Halloween is a rather cool time of year with people dressing up in all kinds of costumes, but are you aware of its origins?

To understand where it comes from, we need to go to Scotland, as it has its roots in the traditional Pagan religion back in ancient history. Back then, it was referred to as All Hallows or All Saints day, with them being celebrated on October 31st. This also then coincided with a very important date for the Celtic religion, which is ancient in its origins. It was a day known as Samhain which roughly translates as 'Feast of the Dead', so you can start to see where it all comes from.

That date was seen in Celtic tradition as being the point where the spirits of the dead could come back to the land of the living for a number of reasons with one of those reasons being to terrify those that were still alive. Ultimately, the two different traditions were combined later on in history to provide us with Halloween, although it is certainly regarded as being less scary and spooky than what it once was thanks to kids going out to trick or treat.

Why Do You Cross One Finger?

There is a pretty good chance that you will have crossed your fingers as a way of believing that it is going to bring you good luck in some way, but are you aware as to the reasons why it is seen as making you luckier?

The origins of this simple gesture are religious in nature, and it is all to do with the cross and asking for divine protection from God. This was originally done in secret, as crossing your fingers to represent the cross had to be done in such a way so as it did not attract the attention of Pagans who would have certainly had something to say about it all in the early days of Christianity.

So, basically the act of crossing your fingers was an attempt to stop bad luck from affecting you more than good luck and it was certainly a protective thing to do. Now, we just relate it to good luck with most people oblivious to its religious beginnings.

What is Your Personal Bubble?

How comfortable do you feel when people are standing a certain distance away from you? This is something that varies from person to person, but are you aware that it is often referred to as your personal bubble?

The average distance will also vary depending on your location, as different cultures have distinct ideas as to what is the perfect personal bubble diameter. For example, people that live in a rural area will have a larger bubble than those that live in a city. This is due to the city-dweller being used to having individuals effectively in their face all of the time with less space available, so it gets to the point where it no longer affects you the same way.

However, if you also compare the difference between two countries, you can see how this is able to become a rather complex matter.

In the United States, the personal bubble space can vary anywhere from 18 to 48 inches, which is a huge difference. However, go to Japan and they have a completely different idea of what amounts to personal space as the average distance is a mere 10 inches. So, when you go to any new place, just spend some time checking out how people stand, as it will have a real impact on your ability to relax when interacting with people.

What are Non-Contact and High-Contact Cultures?

The way in which we interact as human beings can be absolutely fascinating, but there are huge differences in various parts of the world, which does then lead to a certain sense of confusion. Take the concept of non-contact and high-contact cultures. Perhaps you are not even sure as to what they entail, but a quick explanation will certainly suffice.

Basically, it refers to different cultures where there are varying degrees of personal contact, as in some places it is seen as being far more prominent and allowed than it is in other places. Ultimately, it can lead to you freaking out if you are used to virtually no contact and then encounter people that feel as if they are touching you on a constant basis.

Generally speaking, Northern Europe and the Far East are rarely interested in the contact part of socialization, but the complete opposite is true in Latin America, Southern Europe and the Middle East. In those cultures, it is certainly more full-on, but of course it is always in a friendly manner at all times.

So, if you travel to any of those cultures that are the opposite to what you are used to, just remember that different cultures do act in various ways and that it is nothing personal.

Do You Pacify with Your Behavior?

Are you aware of some of the more subtle things that you tend to do with your actions? You probably don't even give them any real thought on the majority of occasions, but perhaps you should as it can open up an entirely new world of possibilities, as well as understanding your own self.

As humans, we are all guilty of displaying certain self-pacifying behavior, and we are talking about small movements that we will often just take for granted. This has been shown in studies to include touching your neck, playing with your hair in some way, or some individuals will even play with their tongue when their mouth is closed.

So, why do we do this? Well, the answer is that these small movements bring us a certain sense of peace, and in the process of doing so it encourages the brain to release endorphins, which are the feel-good chemicals. These chemicals are known to soothe us to such an extent that it then allows us to carry on with what we really want to be doing at that time.

How Old is Your Greenhouse?

Having a greenhouse to help you to cultivate new plants is not actually a relatively new invention. Instead, the origins of this particular structure go further back into history than most people are even aware.

If you had to guess, how old would you say the idea of the greenhouse was? You probably just go back a few centuries, but you would be nowhere near the correct answer.

Instead, you are looking at the greenhouse dating back to roughly 30AD, and it was all thanks to Emperor Tiberius. It seems that he came up with the idea of having to eat an African cucumber every single day, but the climate would not allow that to happen naturally, so his staff had to come up with a way to make sure that the plants could grow throughout the year to prevent the Emperor from becoming irate. Ultimately, it led to something that could easily be identified as the first greenhouse.

In addition, the first greenhouse that was built in the United States appeared in 1737 with it being designed and built by Andrew Faneuil in Boston.

What Caused a Tulip Craze?

The Netherlands are crazy about tulips, but have you ever sat and wondered as to why they are so mad for this particular kind of flower to such an extent that it dominates fields throughout the country? Well, back in 1637, they were still quite popular as a flower, but there was then an incident whereby a virus attacked some of the tulips, which ultimately led to those attacked to change color.

The problem was that people actually believed that a brand-new plant had been discovered, and they then went crazy in trying to obtain this new plant. At the same time, the price for a single tulip bulb increased dramatically because of the rush to own it, so people tried to take advantage of the madness that had surrounded them.

Ultimately, it led to people exchanging things such as 12

sheep for a bulb or a vast amount of grain just to be the owner of this new flower that had apparently hit the market. Imagine how upset they would have been when they discovered that it was just a virus that had changed a flower that they already had, but then the Dutch and their fascination with the tulip persists to this day.

What Makes You More Attractive?

One of the cool things about body language is that it does teach you a whole lot more about how we perceive ourselves and each other. For example, what movement do you feel is able to contribute to people being viewed as more attractive? It is certainly going to be far more subtle than you thought.

People will often think that it is to do with what they are wearing or how they look, and even though that does play a role it, is not the correct answer in this instance. Instead, it has been shown that people that tilt their head just slightly are then perceived to be far more attractive as a direct result. Yes, that one slight movement can alter how people see you, but it is also why some people always seem to do that movement when they are attempting to be 'cute' because they are trying to feed into that feeling.

So, if anybody ever calls you out on it and accuses you of trying to be cute, then tell them that this is not the case and you are actually just being attractive.

Where Does the Term 'Cosmetic' Come From?

The cosmetic industry is one of the biggest in the world today, but even though it does have various branches, are you aware of the origins of the word that described the entire market?

The word 'cosmetic' comes from the Ancient Greeks, who certainly contributed more than their fair share of words to today's the English language, and it stems from their word 'kosmos'. This word is indeed the same as our 'cosmos' but you would never think about putting the two terms together since they describe completely different things.

However, the Greek word itself actually means 'to adorn, to arrange, and to order' so you start to see how it is then applied to makeup and even the concept of cosmetic surgery or cosmetic dentistry. It is clearly linked to the idea of adorning makeup or making changes, which means arranging things differently, until it is to your preference.

How Big is Avon in Brazil?

Everybody knows that Avon is big business, but it seems that in Brazil it is far bigger than so many other things in life that you would like to think were more important. For example, it is estimated that there are around one million people selling Avon in Brazil, and that is more than the number of men and women that they have in both their army and navy combined.

In other words, it is clear that Avon products are deemed as being more important than looking after the safety and security of the entire country, but when you throw in the fact that Brazil is also one of the countries that spends the most on cosmetic surgery, then perhaps it is not such a big surprise as you would like to think.

Would You Do This to Remove Freckles?

There have been different stages in history where having freckles was deemed as being beautiful followed by it being one of those things that you just did not want to have. At this point, it was common for people to go to amazing lengths to try to remove them, but you have to feel that a line had been crossed back in 18th century America when it reached a point that not having freckles was seen as being the fashionable look.

So, what do you think the women of this time would do in an attempt to rid themselves of those freckles? Well, the story goes that they would effectively wash their face with some warm urine, as they believed that this would somehow remove the offending freckles and leave their skin blemish free. Of course, this would not then actually work, meaning they had rubbed urine all over their face for no reason whatsoever, but it was certainly a craze that caught on for a short period of time.

Perhaps using makeup to conceal them is a much better way of achieving a desired end result?

What is the Most Popular Fruit in the World?

Fruit is popular around the world, but do you have any idea as to what the most popular fruit is in terms of how much of it is grown and consumed in a single year? There are a few apparent contenders for the crown, but the majority of people will end up actually getting the answer wrong.

The correct answer is the tomato, and a lot of people end up forgetting that the tomato is indeed a fruit, but it far outstrips its other competitors for the title of the most popular fruit in the world. Not only are there over 10,000 different varieties to choose from, but there are more than 60 million tons of the fruit grown in a single year around the world. That equates to a huge amount of tomatoes that are then used in a variety of ways.

Oh, and the second most popular fruit in the world? The banana, but it just cannot come close to the tomato in terms of popularity or the number of them grown over a 12-month period.

Who was Responsible for the Hanging Gardens of Babylon?

The Hanging Gardens of Babylon are regarded as being one of the seven wonders of the ancient world, but even though so many people have heard of them, a smaller percentage are actually aware of who was responsible for their creation.

The answer lies in the history of a Neo-Babylonian King who went by the name of Nebuchadnezzar II. He was based in what is now known as the Iraqi region of Babil, and that name alone gives you a few hints as to where the name 'Babylon' actually comes from as well.

Even though evidence for it is not as apparent as some of the other ancient wonders, it is still widely believed that they did indeed exist, as it was also common for an ancient King to want to do something that would ultimately make them memorable for eternity. Unfortunately for this King, it seems that even though his creation has effectively stood the test of time, people are rather quick at forgetting his own name, making everything pretty pointless for him.

Why Does Lamborghini Have Such Strange Names?

The supercar manufacturer Lamborghini are not only famous for producing cars that look unlike anything else that is out there on the market, but for also coming up with some rather strange names. However, it all becomes crystal clear when you look more closely at the monikers that they give the different versions, as they are not as crazy as they may have initially appeared.

To better understand what is going on, you have to look at the logo for Lamborghini, which is a bull. Once you realize this, it then all starts to make sense when you then learn that each and every version that they produce is then called after something connected to bullfighting.

For example, the Murcielago and the Diablo effectively pay homage to the names of a couple of famous bulls, while the Estoque refers to the make of sword that a matador uses in his fights. So, basically, the company is merely continuing the links to the world of bulls that appear on their logo.

Your Nails Say It All

If you look at the range of colors of nail polish that are available today, then you are going to find it strange to think about how different it used to be when the idea of nail polish first appeared on the shelves.

It seems that the original patent and production of this product happened back in 1919, and the very first color was classified as a very faint pink. In other words, it was just a subtle difference to our own natural nail color without it being too garish. However, all is not as it initially appears simply because culture and society did manage to largely dictate the colors due to the way in which they were often viewed by many.

For example, the concept of wearing nail polish that was darker than a faint light pink was just something that you were never expected to do. The reason? It was classed as being immoral, and if you were guilty of wearing a dark color, then you would be classed as being the same, which you certainly did not want to happen back in the times between the two world wars. Who knows what those people would think if they saw the wide array of colors that are now available.

Bleeding for Beauty

People are generally aware that individuals will push the absolute limits in an attempt to look beautiful. In the world today, we tend to turn to a wide range of makeup or surgery to get the look that we desire. However, back in history they had far fewer options than what are available today.

Take the 14th century as a perfect example. There was a trend whereby you had to look very pale as that was seen as being the most beautiful look of all, but some women would take things to an absolute extreme to achieve the desired look. It is known that in order to do this, they would use leeches and basically bleed themselves to such an extent that they would lose some of their color and become paler. They would effectively dice with death to achieve what they thought was going to be the desired look.

Of course, some would go too far and lose too much blood, so they would become very pale indeed when they ultimately died as a result of their quest to look beautiful.

What is the Face Platter?

We humans are strange with the way in which we do things, but have you ever heard of the term 'face platter'? If not, then you are not alone, but it is something that you are going to have encountered at some point in your life, of that there is no doubt.

Basically, the face platter is when an individual places their hands on top of one another and then rests their face on their hands. It is called so as it is seen as being akin to your face appearing as if it is indeed on a platter. The idea is that it is supposed to make you look more attractive, and it is something that is primarily used by both women as well as gay men, when they are involved in the art of courtship.

Of course, the success rate does vary a great deal, but it is something that a number of people do without even thinking about it too much. So, the next time you are out and about in a relaxed atmosphere, just take a look around to see how many people are indeed exhibiting the whole face platter approach.

Does Your Lipstick Represent Social Standing?

The entire lipstick thing is more involved than you would think possible, but in this instance, we are neither talking about the range of colors that are out there nor the different types of lipsticks ranging from balms to gloss.

Instead, we are talking about something that has since lost its appeal in society because it used to be the case that the color of lipstick you wore had less to do with what suited your skin color and more the status you held in society.

Back in the times of Ancient Rome, even men would wear lipstick to signify their social standing, and it did then give them a certain amount of respect. On the flip side, people who were lower down in society would not want to go and advertise the fact, so it does mean that there were some people that kind of faked it to preserve their dignity.

So, the next time somebody tells you that the shade of lipstick you are wearing is not doing you justice, let them know that you are merely trying to show off your social standing and then leave them wondering as to what exactly you mean by it all.

Those Civil War Horses were Busy

When you think of the American Civil War, it is common to focus primarily on the men that were involved in the different battles, but there were also a number of horses involved in the conflict. It is estimated that there were in the region of one million horses involved, but that is not the fact that we wish to focus on at this moment in time.

Instead, it is estimated that in a single day, those one million horses would have been able to produce enough urine to fill 12 Olympic swimming pools, which is pretty impressive when you think about it. Of course, you then wonder as to who sat down and worked all of that out as they clearly have more than enough time on their hands.

But also, it makes you think about the logistics that were involved when you had to deal with so many horses on any given day. If you thought that looking after the army was tough enough, then you might now have a better understanding of just how difficult it all was.

Who was the First Person to Die in a Car Accident in the United States?

They say that the odds of being killed in a car accident in the United States is approximately 1:112, but of course go back over 100 years ago and there was less chance of it happening due to there being fewer cars on the road. However, that then opens up the question as to who the first person was to die in a car accident within the United States, and it is going to go back further in time than you had perhaps expected.

The answer takes us to 1899, and the individual in question was Henry Hale Bliss. Mr. Bliss lived in New York City, and it is believed that he was leaving a streetcar when he was then hit by an electric powered cab. Upon impact, the cab managed to crush both his chest and his head with him being killed on the spot. Little did we realize that this would be the first of many deaths, but only the very first one is able to claim any kind of fame from what was a rather unfortunate incident.

Would You Visit the Poison Garden?

A garden is supposed to be a pleasant experience with you being in touch with nature and enjoying all of the different sights and smells that will ultimately surround you. However, there is one garden in the United Kingdom that may not have the same appeal as others that you may prefer to visit.

The reason for that is because this particular spot is known as the Poison Garden, but it is perhaps not as dangerous as you may have initially expected.

It has this name because its main focus is on growing plants that are not as pretty as you would like to have in your very own garden. In fact, it is home to over 100 different plants that could potentially make you very ill or plants that have a habit of killing various insects. If you do plan on visiting, you are not allowed to smell or touch anything due to the potential dangers that are involved, but then would you be that crazy to go ahead and do that anyway?

This is clearly one garden that you should not seek to replicate on your own.

A Fig Might Not Be Vegan

This is going to sound very strange, but the rather humble fig may not be as pleasant or as nice as it likes to make you think. In fact, there are times where a fig can go from being a vegan-based food source to a non-vegan food source, and that in itself is completely strange.

But then, how can a food fluctuate in this way? Well, it seems that the fig is rather different in its approach to growing, and it is less picky when it comes to how it is able to get its food.

The entire issue results when the fig plant is pollinated by a fig wasp. When the wasp lands to do the dirty deed, the plant actually traps the wasp, and enzymes contained within the plant break down the wasp and basically devour it, using the wasp itself as a food source. According to the strict rules that are associated with vegan food groups, this does mean that it is not vegan, but then you have to know if it has managed to eat any wasps as it grew.

What Terms are Fruits and Vegetables?

There are obvious differences between fruits and vegetables, but the terms themselves do mean that there are even bigger differences than you may have initially understood. In fact, the terms come from two completely different industries.

Fruit is considered a botanical term, whereas vegetable is a culinary term, and yet the two of them come together to form a staple part of our diet. However, if you want to display your knowledge to others, then the actual explanation of the differences between the two does become far more involved.

Basically, a fruit is referred to as being a seed-bearing part of the plant that comes from the ovary of the flower. On the

140

other hand, a vegetable is formed from other parts of the plant, including the leaves, the stems and even the roots.

What then makes it even more complicated is that people tend to associate fruit with being sweet in taste, and then you have fruits such as peppers, the tomato, and eggplant that are not actually sweet. As a result, they are viewed as being vegetables by different chefs around the world, even though that is not strictly true according to their botanical origins.

How Many Copies of the Bible are Sold Each Year?

It is fair to say that the Bible is still a very popular book, but are you aware of just how many copies are still sold each and every year? The answer is going to be rather surprising for you, as there are at least 100 million copies still being sold around the world on a yearly basis. Unsurprisingly, this means that it is one of the most popular books in terms of numbers being sold even after this period of time.

Of course, that number does also include the fact that it is sold in various languages as well as slightly different versions, but when you add it all up, it does come to something that is seriously impressive.

Actually, the Bible has been fully translated into over 500 different languages and partly translated into over 2,500 different languages, as this includes regional dialects and even into more ancient languages that are not really spoken by that many people in the world today.

How Big a Problem was the Black Death?

The Black Death that swept across Europe in the 14th century did indeed wreak absolute havoc on the population. Of course, this was the part of the world that was the most populated at the time, so it also meant that a huge percentage of the entire global population were affected by this disease.

But then, how big a problem was it?

Well, even though we do not have exact figures at hand, it is estimated that as much as two-thirds of the population of Europe at the time died as a direct result of the disease. Even if the idea of 66% of people seems to be high, the vast majority of the studies that have been carried out into the plague do tend to put the average at more than 50%, which is still pretty impressive—in a horrible way.

Also, if you want to put this percentage into real numbers, the estimates vary even more widely due to the way in which the population was spread across the continent. However, even with that, the figure can be as high as 200 million people or as low as 75 million, but even then, you are looking at a large number of people in comparison to population figures at the time.

This was not even the only time that the plague swept into Europe, but it was certainly the point where it really did take its toll, and Europe as a whole was viewed as being quite lucky to even recover from it in the way that it did.

Do You Know Why Italy is Called Italy?

Understanding the way in which different countries get their names can be rather interesting, and Italy is one such example.

The name itself comes from the Italian word 'Italia', but that actually translates as 'calf land', which is only going to confuse matters even more. However, in order to understand why it has this name, we only have to look at the southern part of Italy as that is where we are going to find the answer.

Apparently, the bull was regarded as being an important symbol to tribes that were based in the south of the country. When different tribes ultimately united to create what we now know as Italy, it seems that they were the more vocal and were able to at least keep some reference to their own heritage in the creation of the new country. It also makes you wonder what the other options could have been.

Bodies as Missiles

Warfare from centuries ago was certainly different to how we experience it now. It seems that there have also been times where individuals have been more than willing to use anything that they could get their hands on in order to try to attack their enemy, but this time it could be argued that things just went a bit too far.

In 1347, the Tartars were laying siege to the city of Kaffa, and the inhabitants were understandably becoming rather fed up with the entire scenario. It was also a time when the plague was across the entire area, but it seems that the Tartars had a different idea as to how to effectively take control of the city.

As the city itself had been cut off, it meant that the plague was not such a big deal as it was in other parts of Europe. The Tartars were also open to trying anything that they could to win, so they then came up with the idea to use the bodies of those that had died from the plague as missiles.

In doing so, they basically threw the bodies into the city, which was a blatant attempt to try to get the plague into the confines of the city knowing that people were effectively living on top of one another. It was something that would ultimately work, as people in the city did eventually die from the plague, and in the process of doing so it reduced the level of resistance against the Tartars.

How Does Eyeshadow Glimmer?

When you look at eyeshadow, you will see that there is often a glimmer to it, and yet you may not even be aware of the way in which this effect is achieved. Well, there are several methods that are used in the cosmetics industry that result in the same outcome, but there is one method that is seen as being the most popular. The only problem is that it does make you wonder about what you are putting on your skin when you discover what the key ingredient actually is.

You see, there is a tendency for them to use something called guanine to add the shimmer and glimmer to not only eyeshadow but also lipsticks. Now, at first you might think that the mention of this guanine is not that bad. It certainly sounds as if it would not cause you any problems, but then you probably have no idea what guanine is since you will have never heard of it before.

Well, it is actually fish scales, and if you have just put on some lipstick that has a touch of glimmer about it, then it is perfectly understandable if you feel like washing it off immediately. However, it is not going to do you any harm whatsoever, as they have hardly scraped it off the fish and just thrown it into the mixture. The only other problem is that it will make you wonder as to what else they include in makeup that you are not aware of.

What is the Coldest Temperature Ever Recorded?

There are parts of the world that can end up getting pretty cold at various times of the year, but are you aware of just how cold the earth has been able to get at different points?

You may not be surprised to discover that the coldest

144

temperature that has ever been recorded happened in Antarctica, as it is hardly known as being a tropical paradise. However, the temperature itself would drive you absolutely insane if you had been unfortunate enough to encounter it, even from the warmth of a research hut.

The location in Antarctica was at the Vostock Station, and it occurred in 1983. The temperature was recorded as being -123 Celsius, which is seriously cold. There is no guarantee that it has been the lowest temperature to have ever happened on the earth, but it is certainly the coldest that science has been fortunate enough to record.

How Old is Caffeine?

Caffeine could arguably be the thing that keeps the world spinning, as so many people need their fix of it before they are able to function in the morning. However, do you know how old the use of caffeine is within our society?

Most people would argue that it was just a few centuries old, but you would be so wide of the mark if you did indeed go ahead and give that answer. Instead, archaeologists believe that the use of caffeine goes back to the Palaeolithic age to a date that is approximately 700,000 years ago.

The reason why this theory is believed to be plausible is simply because caffeine appears in a variety of plants, and it has been shown through research that those plants were used all those years ago, so it is hardly a giant leap in the imagination to then decide that our ancient ancestors were also using it like some kind of drug.

Now, they were not using it in the form of coffee or a soft drink, but there is a firm belief that they spent their time chewing on the plant which would still release some of the caffeine into their bloodstream. From this, they would then have more energy to go and hunt for food, so it would have certainly been beneficial for them to make full use of those plants whenever they could.

You Don't Actually Need Caffeine to Start the Day

People often believe that they are unable to start the day until they have had their first coffee, but the truth of the matter is that this is the wrong thing for us to do.

Instead, when we wake, our brain is already very active at helping us to get our energy levels up to a point where we feel that we can actually function. It does this by releasing cortisol that then floods our system. This cortisol is a natural stimulant that does indeed help to fire us up for the difficult day ahead, so our body does not need the caffeine in the way that we believe.

However, if you still feel that this should be part of your morning ritual, then the best way in which you can feel the absolute benefits of it is to wait until later in the morning before you go ahead and have that cup. You will feel that it helps you more than if you had consumed your first coffee as early as possible.

That Cure has a Bad Smell

If you go back several centuries, medical advice and knowledge was certainly far more primitive than it is today, but that is not something that we should ridicule people for. Instead, it makes more sense to try to understand the reasons behind some of their apparent cures, especially when you discover that they did not do anything for those that were ill.

146

Take this as a prime example.

Throughout history, there have been several outbreaks of the plague, and each time there were different attempts to create a cure even though the knowledge that they had regarding the disease was very limited. One theory that seems to have been able to hang around for some time was that bad smells could effectively drive away the plague.

Of course, the mere thought of a bad smell being so powerful to cure the plague is completely bizarre to us, but to the people of the time it made so much sense. It ultimately meant that some of the cures that were thrown around included the use of both urine and animal dung due to the stench that it was able to produce. The only problem was that there was no way that it could cure the disease, and it was actually more likely to result in helping the plague to spread amongst the population.

So, the next time your doctor suggests something that is a bit different as a cure, just stop and think if it is making sense or if it sounds far too strange to be true.

What is the Worst Political Slogan Ever?

The problem with politics and standing for election is that you need to come up with a pretty good slogan that has the ability of making you stand out from the crowd. However, it is not always as easy as you think, and there are occasions where it has gone very wrong indeed for the candidate.

But then, what do you think is the worst slogan ever created for a US Presidential election?

The answer is widely accepted to be that this accolade goes to Al Smith, who was standing for election during the period of time known as the Prohibition. He was firmly against the idea of the Prohibition, and it formed a central part of his entire campaign that he would overturn things if he was successful.

Of course, this all sounds like a good idea and something that he could hold onto, but he then made a massive error when he came up with his slogan. It said as follows: 'Vote for Al Smith and he'll make your wet dreams come true.'

Now, this was not some kind of joke nor a prank being played on him, as it was a very real and a very serious slogan that he had created. The only problem is that it generally does not read as being something that you would then associate with alcohol, so it certainly did not help him to be seen as being a serious candidate for office.

Introducing the Hornet Bomb

The Mayan civilization existed in the area that we now know as Mexico, and they were often regarded as being quite fierce when it came to battle. However, it does seem to be the case that they were willing to try a number of different tactics in an attempt to gain the upper hand.

In order to do so, it seems that the Maya would literally use anything that they had to hand as a weapon, but one of their favorite things was known as a hornet bomb. Now, you can probably make an educated guess as to what this weapon involves, but it does mean that they were using nature in a brand-new way.

Basically, they would take a hornet's nest and throw it as a weapon knowing that the hornets inside would go crazy and start attacking the enemy. They would then be in a panic to such an extent that it would be easier for the Maya to go ahead and defeat them due to the distractions. It may have been basic, and it may not have been pretty, but it was certainly quite effective and something that worked.

Where Does Money Come From?

Money. We all want more of it due to the way in which it changes our lives, but have you ever taken the time to find out where this all-important word comes from? As with a number of things in the English language, we have to go back to the time of the Romans to discover the root, and in doing so we see that they were pretty clued up with what they were doing when it came to coming up with the names for things.

In the Roman period, they would strike all of their coins in a temple that was dedicated to the Goddess Juno Moneta. She was also the Goddess for marriage and women, but her last name would then be associated with the concept of money, as well as us taking the concept of coins being 'minted' from the same source.

The Eagle on the Silver Dollar

Whenever you look at a silver Dollar, then you are going to lay eyes on the image of an eagle, but what a lot of people do not know is that this image is based on an actual real eagle that went by the name of Peter. Yes, it is hardly imaginative, but then getting your image on a coin is pretty cool.

The way in which he came to appear on the coin is more straightforward than you would initially think. Between the years of 1830 and 1835, he was largely adopted by the people that worked at the Mint and basically provided a model for their drawings. Even when he died he was stuffed and is still there on display in the Mint to this very day.

So, whenever you have that silver Dollar in your possession, at least now you can tell anybody that is willing to listen about Peter.

Which Drug is Most Widely Used?

Drugs are bad for you due to their addictive properties as well as the way in which they can destroy lives. Obviously, there are a number of different types of drugs out there for you to choose from, but it then opens up the question as to which drug is the most widely used in the world today?

The answer is far easier than your mind was probably allowing you to consider, as the actual answer is caffeine, which is streets ahead of alcohol in second place and nicotine in third. Of course, this is because of our reliance on not only coffee but also sodas that have a tendency to contain so much caffeine pushed into them that they too have their very own addictive properties.

It wasn't always like this. There was a time when nicotine was higher up the list, and caffeine was certainly not as popular as it is today. To be honest, we can blame the likes of the big-name coffee chains for the way that things have turned out alongside just one or two beverage companies that have dominated the world with their addictive caffeine-based drinks.

How Many Deaths Do People Believe Happened in the Bible?

Even though there are clearly no definitive numbers available, there are various Biblical scholars that have sought to gather together the different evidence for the number of deaths that appear in the various books. Of course, this then leads to a lot

150

of scholarly debate, but the figures that get the most attention are rather scary to say the least.

You see, they have not only sought to compile the deaths, but they have also looked at ways to attribute them to entities. The scholars believe that God was responsible for 25 million deaths while Satan was responsible for 60. Also, they argue that 10 out of the 60 should not even really count, as they are connected to the book of Job where God practically offers a bet to Satan. In other words, some people feel that 25 million is not enough, so they just want to add another ten.

What this shows is that there are some rough times in the Bible, especially if you spend any time paying close attention to the words and passages. If we are honest, even if the figure was not actually 25 million, you can guarantee that it will still be substantially higher than you ever thought possible.

What is the Bloodiest Battle in History?

Even though we could look at World War I or World War II as a whole, and state that they were both bloody battles, we are looking more closely at individual battles that took place. So, when you bring things down to a narrower field, which battle is actually the bloodiest in not only history connected to either war, but in history in general?

The answer is the Battle of Stalingrad, and this was nothing more than an absolute massacre. Even though there are no exact numbers, it is accepted that there were a minimum of 800,000 casualties, and the figure may have actually been as high as 1.6 million. It must be noted that this is related solely to the number of casualties resulting directly from the war itself and not through normal disease, but it does show how nobody really wanted to fight this battle as the chances of coming out on the other side-without injuries did appear to be relatively slim.

Keeping People Out of the Vatican

The Vatican City has a number of unique claims to fame, but one of the lesser known facts is the way in which it is able to guard itself. You see, this is the only country in the world that is able to protect itself at night by simply closing and locking the gates. In doing so, the entire country, well there are just over 107 acres in the country, is sealed off from the rest of the world.

Of course, you can imagine that it would be extremely difficult for any other country to be able to do this due to the sheer scale and size of the wall and gates that would be required. This is obviously something that has been left alone for centuries, but even though they do not actively go ahead and close the gates in this way, it still remains an option.

Soda and Getting Older

People are largely aware that drinking a lot of soda is not exactly going to be good for your health, but there is one fact that is going to probably stop you in your tracks.

This fact is that if you drink one can of soda per day, it is going to age you by approximately 4.6 years. In other words, drinking soda on a regular basis is going to put years on you, and that is not exactly a good thing.

It is all to do with the sugar, caffeine, and other key ingredients that are contained within the drink as to the reason why this happens. There are so many things in soda that our body then struggles to deal with that it leads to an increased risk of diabetes, weight gain, and a number of other health issues that are not going to be beneficial to you.

When you add all of this together, it then means that soda can indeed add some years to your current physical age, so if you are serious about longevity, then cutting back on your soda consumption may very well be the correct way to go.

Watch Out, Your Soda is on Fire

One of the interesting things about the world is the way in which different ingredients are allowed in some countries and yet they are banned in others. One such example involves an ingredient that appears in a number of different sodas that are available for sale in the United States.

However, when you look at the ingredient and why it is banned in some places, it does make you wonder as to why it's still used as a key ingredient in drinks such as Dr. Pepper and Sprite, to name only a couple.

The ingredient in question is known as BVO, which is short for Brominated Vegetable Oil. At first it sounds as if it would be absolutely acceptable, as we use vegetable oil in a number of different things, but your attitude will change when you discover that this ingredient is actually toxic and is used as a basis in at least one type of flame retardant. It is banned throughout Europe as well as Japan, but the same ban has not been extended to the United States where it still has a certain popularity.

How Many Types of Tea Do You Believe Exists?

Even though it falls some distance behind coffee in the popularity stakes, tea is still consumed on a vast scale on a daily basis. However, do you know how many different types of tea are actually in existence at this moment in time?

The answer is a staggering 1,500 different varieties, and they each have their own unique taste to them. Also, we are not talking about different teas blended together to create something else, but instead this covers teas that are restricted to certain areas, unique growing conditions, taste, strength, and a whole host of other things.

In general, the tea that you buy in a store is going to often be a poor reflection of what is actually out there, and it would be almost impossible to track down examples of each and every variety to decide which your favorite is. Furthermore, China is the country that is responsible for producing the most tea in a single year, with India coming as a distant second, which is something that often surprises individuals since Indian teas tend to be the most well-known.

What is the Difference in Water Usage Between Africa and the United States?

Okay, so we know that large swathes of Africa have issues with gathering together enough water for them to survive, but if you want to get a good idea of just how big a difference there is between people in Africa compared to people in the United States, then there is one way of doing it.

That way is to contrast the average daily consumption of water because the difference goes beyond being crazy. In general, the average African family will make do with 23L of water a day. This is nothing compared to the average American family and how much water they use in various ways over the same time period. It is believed that the figure is as high as 950L of water per day thanks to laundry, cleaning, showering, and other things that we just take for granted.

So, the next time that you are accused of wasting water, then just remember that you are always going to be doing that anyway in comparison to people in Africa.

How Long Does It Take for a Plastic Bottle to Decompose?

The problem with plastic bottles is that they are everywhere. If you look at landfill, each one is full of these bottles as they have become such a mainstay of our lives.

However, even though they are inexpensive to produce and therefore make it cheaper for us to buy the contents within the bottles, there is still a price to pay. That price is connected to what happens if we do not look at trying to recycle as much as possible because it can end up being a blight on our landscape for longer than you would imagine.

Due to the structure of the plastic that is used in the bottle, it is not the kind of thing that can be broken down very quickly by nature doing its own thing. In fact, it has been calculated that the plastic bottles we are using today could take as long as 500 years for them to decompose naturally, and with the growing number of them being used, that is going to lead to a major problem.

So, when you are using plastic bottles, try to recycle them, or we will get to a point where we cannot see what we are doing because of being surrounded by massive heaps of these bottles.

How Much More Expensive is Bottled Water Compared to Tap Water?

The bottled water market continues to grow at a crazy rate,

but have you ever stopped to think about just how much more expensive bottled water is in comparison to the tap water variety? The answer is astonishing.

Considering the technology that is used to get the water out of the ground, put through different processes, and then bottled, it is no surprise that the bottled version is indeed far more expensive. In fact, it has been concluded that bottled water can be between 600 and 3,700 times more expensive by the gallon in comparison to tap water. Now, when you stop and think about that fact, then you need to start to question as to whether or not it is indeed worth all of that extra money.

What is the Complete Name of Pablo Picasso?

Pablo Picasso is one of the greatest artists to have ever lived and was responsible for the creation of a brand-new movement. Most people believe that this is his complete name, but if you were one of those people, you would be wrong.

Instead, his full name consists of 23 different words, which refer to a range of family members as well as different saints. It was quite common for some families to effectively compile a list in this way as they believed that it would lead to that individual being blessed in their life. You would have to say that it did kind of work in the case of Picasso when you think of the kind of life that he then went on to lead.

So, what is this name? Deep breath as it does go on for an eternity.

Pablo Diego Jose Francisco de Paula Juan Nepomuceno Maria de los Remedios Cipriano de la Santisima Trinidad Martyr Patricio Clito Ruiz y Picasso.

Was Cocaine Ever Sold on the Open Market?

People are aware of the fact that cocaine is a deadly drug that is sold through a series of clandestine meetings and often for a high price, but it has not always been that way. Instead, if you go back into the 19th century, then you will find that there were parts of the United States where it was actually being sold as one of the key cures for a number of different ailments and limitations.

The year was 1885, and a manufacturer in the United States was responsible for doing something that we now recognize as being the craziest thing that a company could do. They stated that their cocaine would do wonderful things for individuals, including making them feel brave and immune to pain. It was certainly something that appealed to so many people, but ultimately we discovered the true impact it has on individuals, which then meant that it was no longer as popular as the manufacturer had hoped it would be.

What are the Origins of Chess?

Chess is a popular board game that has its roots firmly set in ancient history, but even though it has been around for some time, the origins of the game are something that most people are unaware of. In most cases, people tend to point towards China as being its place of birth, but if you thought that as well, you would be wrong.

Instead, we have to travel to India to discover its origins because even the name of the game comes from that part of the world. It all stems from a Sanskrit word 'chaturanga', which roughly translated means 'four members of an army' and even though it started off in a different form to how we play it today, most experts say that this was the first version.

Apparently, the game referred to foot soldiers, chariots, horses, and elephants, so it did have to go through a few adaptations to get to the version that we are familiar with today. It is believed that the game spread from India into what is now Iran before it was readily accepted in the Muslim world, which sped up the rate that it spread. After that, it made its way into Southern Europe, and the rest truly is history, as it quickly became a game that would end up extending to the rest of the world.

The Meaning of the Himalayas

Most people are aware that the highest mountain range in the world is the Himalayas. It runs through India and Nepal, as well as parts of China, but what does the name 'Himalayas' actually translate into?

For that, we need to look at the Sanskrit language for an answer, and in doing so we have to split it up into two sections 'hima' and 'alaya' in order to get our answer. With this, we then see that 'hima' means 'snow' while 'alaya' means 'abode'. So, as you can see, it's not as complicated an answer as you were perhaps expecting. In fact, it is actually very descriptive when you think that the mountains are indeed a snow abode.

Of course, Nepal and China have their own versions of the names, but it is the name, Himalayas, that has been able to make its mark in the English-speaking world.

What are the Roots of Modern Day Vegetarianism?

The idea of being vegetarian is certainly something that has increased in popularity in recent years, but do you know the roots of what has become known as modern-day vegetarianism?

The answer is, perhaps not surprisingly, India.

Vegetarianism has been a staple part of Indian life for centuries with its origins in religious texts whereby animals were often regarded as being sacred. Also, there was a monetary issue connected to it since meat was expensive, whereas the poor could grow their own vegetables or had a better chance of purchasing them.

Even though the Indian economy is more stable today, it also accounts for the biggest percentage of vegetarians in the world. It is believed that as many as 70% of all vegetarians are in India, so if you are seeking any kind of inspiration as to the different vegetarian dishes you should be experimenting with, then looking at Indian cooking would certainly be advisable.

How Much Money was Lost on Black Tuesday?

The Great Depression was horrific for anybody that was involved in it, but are you aware of just how much money was lost on that all important Black Tuesday? You need to remember that we are talking about something that is getting close to 100 years ago, so the amount of money from then would pale into insignificance if you apply today's current rates.

However, it you forget about that part, then the money that was lost is truly astonishing.

On that one single day, the Wall Street markets lost a staggering $14 billion, and throughout that week they lost a total of $30 billion. Today, we are talking about crazy numbers if you convert that into our current economy and the present-day monetary value of things, as it would be approximately $370 billion. If that kind of thing happened today, we could end up being in another major depression, which is no surprise when the markets basically crashed in a matter of hours.

But then, there are some economists that argue the depression itself was not caused by this crash in the markets. Instead, the blame is put firmly at the feet of the countless individuals that ran to their banks and withdrew their money in a panic. That money drained the banks, meaning they could not rally against the crashes, and what would have been an economic blip turned into something horrific that lasted for years.

Walt Disney and Menstruation

Everybody is used to Walt Disney producing cartoons and movies for children that allow them to just drift off into a fantasy world, but do you think that it would even be possible for Walt Disney to produce something in relation to menstruation?

It does sound crazy, but it is actually true, and the fact that he did something connected to it back in 1946 is equally as astonishing.

The movie was very factual, as it was an attempt to explain some of the issues surrounding menstruation, and it was probably also the very first movie that had ever used the word 'vagina.' You would hardly have expected the first movie to use that word to have come from Walt Disney, as that is the last person that should have ventured anywhere near there.

How Many Tampons Will a Woman Use in Her Lifetime?

Considering the number of years that a woman will menstruate, it's no surprise that they are going to use a substantial number of tampons throughout their life. However, with that point in mind, it is still an estimation as to the average number that will be used, even though the end result is going to be pretty surprising.

On average, a woman is going to use a total of 11,400 tampons in her lifetime, and that is certainly a figure that is going to be far above what you would expect. This does vary a lot, but even if that figure is 2,000 tampons out, that is still a lot to purchase throughout a lifetime.

However, this figure would drop if you were alive in Prehistoric times, as women then only menstruated a fraction of the number of times due to a shorter life expectancy. Also, women that live in an agrarian society are also known to menstruate around half as many times as women in the western world.

Would a Wolf Make a Good Guard Dog?

Considering the reputation that they have, you would automatically assume that a wolf would make a wonderful guard dog and that nobody would venture anywhere near your home or whatever it was they were protecting. However, if that is indeed what you thought, then you would be very, very wrong.

Instead, a wolf would actually make a horrible guard dog, and it is all due to something that people either do not know or seem to gloss over for any number of reasons. You see, a wolf is known to actually be terrified of things that are unknown to them. In other words, if they were guarding an area and heard something that they did not understand, then they would have a tendency to run in the complete opposite direction. This is hardly what you want your guard dog to do.

A wolf is tough to see simply because it will not even bark at an intruder since it is too busy running away, so they are perhaps not as fierce as they are reported to be in the media. Oh, and if you thought that you could sneak up on them, then you would be incorrect because they can hear noises up to six miles away and have developed over 200 million scent cells, whereas us humans have a mere five million.

What is the Legend of the Black Eyes on a Panda?

Who doesn't love the Black Panda? However, even though it is famous for having black patches around its eyes, are you aware of the legend that lies behind them?

The story itself may appear to be slightly unconventional, but then isn't any legend? Basically, the tale behind it is that the panda was originally completely white in color. A young girl stumbled across a panda cub that was being attacked by a leopard, and she could not stand back and just allow this to happen. Unfortunately for her, the leopard stopped attacking the cub and killed her instead.

After this, pandas came to her funeral and wore armbands that were made from black sashes. Sad at what had happened, the pandas began to cry, and in trying to wipe away the tears, the pandas inadvertently smudging the sashes over their eyes. It then led to their eyes becoming stained leading to the familiar look that we all know and love today.

What is the Fastest Bear in the World?

Bears have a habit of being very scary, but there is an additional fact about them that does make them even scarier than ever before. That fact is the speed at which they can run, because if you are unlucky enough to encounter one, then you better hope that luck is on your side.

While a bear such as the panda is slow, and you could outrun it quite easily, the pace of the brown bear is something completely different. The difficulty for you with a brown bear is that they can reach speeds as high as 35mph, which is the same speed attained by the average horse. Now, it's a pretty good guess that it would be impossible for you to outrun something that is going at that speed, so you better hope that the bear has a muscle injury of some kind to give you a fighting chance.

A Guinea Pig is Not a Pig

Even though its name appears to hint at it, the guinea pig is not a pig, nor is it even in the same family. Instead, it is classified as a rodents, and not even originally from the country of Guinea either. Its place of origin is the Andes in South America.

So, if it is not actually part of the pig family, then why does it have that name?

Well, there are several potential reasons as to why this is the case. Some people argue that it is entirely due to the way in which it squeals like a pig, while others claim it is because it is built like a pig even though it is in a much smaller fashion. To those that argue this point, it is because it has no real tail, a short neck, and when compared to the rest of its body, the neck is quite large just like a pig's.

For the Guinea part, there is a theory that it actually relates to the guinea pig potentially being sold for the price of one Guinea, which was an old monetary coin that is now out of use. Of course, they cost a bit more than that today.

Why Does Rudolph Have a Red Nose?

Rudolph is probably the most well-known celebrity in the world that has a red nose, but why does he appear to have been afflicted with this? Well, it seems that scientists in Norway have a bit too much time on their hands as they have spent time trying to work out what exactly is going on with his nose. However, maybe all of their hard work is not in vain, as they have claimed that they have indeed managed to come up with something.

According to the scientists, they state that it would be most likely caused by a parasitic infection in the nasal area. Yep, it really is as boring as that, but then what else did you expect? The problem is that it would hardly make for a good Christmas story if it had to include the term 'parasitic infection.'

Mistletoe Might Not Be as Nice as You Think

When it comes to something that is romantic, kissing under the mistletoe must be right up there with roses on Valentine's Day. However, you might change your mind when you find out something else about the plant.

The name comes from an old Anglo-Saxon word 'mistletan' so you can already see the similarities, but it's when you look at the translation that things take a rather unfortunate turn. The problem with this word is that it means 'little dung twig' because the plant is able to spread by its fruit being eaten by birds who then dispose of it from the opposite end of their mouth in their droppings. Of course, that was not the reason why it became a sacred plant. That lies with the Druids who saw it staying green even in winter when other plants were dead.

Also, the plant grew berries providing a source of food for different birds and animals, so it was then interpreted as being a life-giver plant with a touch of luck attached to it as well. Ultimately, it went through several changes in its interpretation to then lead to how we think of it today, which is as a plant that is supposed to bring love and luck to the couples that kiss beneath it.

DON'T FORGET YOUR FREE BOOKS

GET THEM FOR FREE ON
WWW.TRIVIABILL.COM

MORE BOOKS BY BILL O'NEILL

I hope you enjoyed this book and learned something new. Please feel free to check out some of my previous books on **Amazon**.

Printed in Great Britain
by Amazon

32995263R00106